And Why Not?

STUDIES IN ETHICS AND ECONOMICS

Series Editor
Samuel Gregg, Acton Institute

Economics as a discipline cannot be detached from a historical background that was, it is increasingly recognized, religious in nature. Adam Ferguson and Adam Smith drew on the work of sixteenth- and seventeenth-century Spanish theologians, who strove to understand the process of exchange and trade in order to better address the moral dilemmas they saw arising from the spread of commerce in the New World. After a long period in which economics became detached from theology and ethics, many economists and theologians now see the benefit of studying economic realities in their full cultural, often religious, context. This new series, Studies in Ethics and Economics, provides an international forum for exploring the difficult theological and economic questions that arise in the pursuit of this objective.

Titles in the Series

Intelligence as a Principle of Public Economy / Del pensiero come principio d'economia publica, by Carlo Cattaneo
And Why Not?: The Human Person at the Heart of Business, by François Michelin
Faith and Liberty: The Economic Thought of the Late Scholastics, by Alejandro A. Chafuen
The Boundaries of Technique: Ordering Positive and Normative Concerns in Economic Research, by Andrew Yuengert
Within the Market Strife: American Economic Thought from Rerun Novarum *to Vatican II,* by Kevin E. Schmiesing
Natural Law: The Foundation of an Orderly Economic System, by Alberto M. Piedra

And Why Not?

The Human Person at the Heart of Business

François Michelin

An Interview with
Ivan Levaï and Yves Messarovitch

Translated by
Mark Sebanc

LEXINGTON BOOKS
Lanham • Boulder • New York • Toronto • Oxford

LEXINGTON BOOKS

Published in the United States of America
by Lexington Books
An imprint of The Rowman & Littlefield Publishing Group, Inc.
4501 Forbes Boulevard, Suite 200, Lanham, Maryland 20706

PO Box 317
Oxford
OX2 9RU, UK

British Library Cataloguing in Publication Information Available

Library of Congress Cataloging-in-Publication Data

Michelin, François.
  [Et pourquoi pas? English]
  And why not?: the human person at the heart of business / François Michelin; an
interview with Ivan Levaï and Yves Messarovitch; translated by Marc Sebanc.
    p. cm.
  Includes index.
  ISBN 0-7391-0542-6 (cloth: alk. paper) — ISBN 0-7391-0543-4 (pbk.: alk. paper)
  1. Pneu Michelin (Firm). 2. Michelin, François—Interviews. 3. Executives—
France—Interviews. 4. Social responsibility of business—France. 5. International
economic relations. I. Levaï, Ivan. II. Messarovitch, Yves. III. Title.
HD9161.5.T574P64513 2003
338.0944'092—dc21   2002043445

Printed in the United States of America

⊖™ The paper used in this publication meets the minimum requirements of American
National Standard for Information Sciences—Permanence of Paper for Printed Library
Materials, ANSI/NISO Z39.48–1992.

To my wife, Bernadette, and to our children.

CONTENTS

FOREWORD

Many men and women of faith not only understand the creative genius of the free enterprise system, but they also live it. In this way, they engage their vocation as an entrepreneur in a way that is illuminated by an awareness of the grandeur that lies beyond this life and that also gives ultimate meaning to the present.

The subject of this book is indeed one of those individuals. For several decades, François Michelin has exercised the creativity of his mind to see what others have not seen and to go where others have yet to tread. In the world of business, he has been an explorer into the unknown, with the gift of insight into the real potential that lies dormant within the world that God has created. The moral and material flourishing that has resulted from Michelin's lifelong quest is indeed astounding. Not only has it transformed the world of the automobile industry, but Michelin's work has also helped to allow ordinary men and women to know and to see that they are part of a complex yet fruitful process that lifts others out of poverty and allows humanity to expand to the horizons of its possibilities.

At first glance, François Michelin would not cause such lofty thoughts to arise in one's mind. In many senses, Michelin is a simple man. His personal tastes are quiet and unassuming, and in terms of appearance, there is little to distinguish him from many of his fellow Frenchmen. Lacking the desire to court attention from the press, Michelin is quite simply rather unfazed by the trappings of wealth.

What emerges, however, from this series of interviews is a man who has thoroughly integrated his profession as a business leader with an appreciation of the high moral demands of his occupation. Moreover, Michelin is not afraid to place his thought and work in the context of philosophical and theological reflection. As becomes clear, Michelin has clearly embraced a set of principles. At the same time, he allows his mind to range across the intellectual landscape and to ask questions that many in contemporary France, indeed, much of the West, would prefer to ignore. Why, he asks, do those with entrepreneurial ability constantly find themselves unduly restrained by the State as well as by collectivist avatars from Europe's past? And why, Michelin wonders, do so many politicians and intellectuals still think in discredited Marxist categories when it comes to thinking about the nature of economic life?

As Michelin explores these and other questions through a process of respectful but pointed dialogue with his interlocutors, what emerges is a conviction is that man is, as a pope once famously put it, man's gift to man. In the individual person, Michelin sees a being designed to transform both himself and the world from what they are into what they ought to be. Apart from sin, the greatest obstacle to such transformation is, in Michelin's view, those ideologies that rely upon visions of man as mere consumers of goods as well as upon myths about free enterprise that have little to do with reality and owe more to the novels of Charles Dickens.

In theological terms, the reader will soon discern that Michelin is making a particular appeal in these interviews for the Christian Church to comprehend the creativity and dynamism of the entrepreneur and the free enterprise system, instead of simply unthinkingly joining the chorus of condemnation that private enterprise regularly encounters. Michelin is clearly a man of spirituality that, for him, is as natural as the process by which his business turns raw elements of the earth into products that truly serve the human person. He is, however, troubled by the fact that many who share his belief in God do not share these insights into the religious dimension of entrepreneurial activity.

Being a humble man, Michelin believes in discussing these thoughts in a respectful way with others: Witness his account of his willingness to engage in a dialogue with a Marxist trade unionist. Michelin also evidently believes that many of his fellow believers, perhaps especially theologians and clergy, need to reflect anew upon that part of the truth that is to be found in the realm of economics and to integrate it into their ongoing search for understanding of man's place in the cosmos.

Hence, as readers join this dialogue with Michelin and his interlocutors as silent participants, they would be well-advised to keep in mind that this is a man who is ultimately concerned with higher things, but who sees their meaning made real in the apparently ordinary happenings of everyday business life. Herein lies the beauty of this text. It allows that which is, in some respects, beyond human comprehension to become manifest to the human mind. While they may maintain some elements of a mystery, we should remember that mysteries are not things that are completely impenetrable to man but, rather, realities into which man has some insight without enjoying complete understanding. In these interviews, François Michelin helps the relationship between the terrestrial and the transcendent to become more apparent and, thus, renders a service to all.

—Sir John Templeton
October 28, 2002

FOREWORD

François Michelin—A Gentleman

François Michelin is a most unlikely top executive. "He is a real gentleman!" maintains his neighbor Michel Charasse, a former minister under François Mitterand but now mayor of Puy-Guillaume[1] and a Socialist senator from Puy de Dôme.[2]

François Michelin is indeed a real gentleman. All you have to do is step out with him to the offices he has in Clermont and Breteuil Avenue in Paris, or to one of his factories, to measure the respect that this gentleman commands quite naturally and unaffectedly when he crosses paths with a secretary, an engineer, or a worker. The boss and his employee greet one another, looking each other clearly in the eye in a spirit of mutual esteem, without any hint of phoniness, just the way it must have happened in yesteryear between people living in the same village.

Even at seventy-two years of age, Mr. François, as people call him as a token of their esteem, is a fine figure of a man. With frank, lively eyes and white hair, his long strides and the distinct way he bows his head in thought are reminiscent of Jacques Tati in his role as Mr. Hulot.[3]

How did the two of us make contact with this man, who is so very discreet? For one of us, it was a radio program that precipitated the first meeting, while for the other it was *Le Figaro*.[4]

A ravenous consumer of interesting personalities, inasmuch as he was seeing them at the rate of one a day as part of his "Explain Yourself" radio program on Europe 1, Ivan Levaï took it into his head one morning to invite onto his show the most reserved, the least media-oriented of French top executives, namely, François Michelin.

"That was twenty years ago. A polite request was made to the chairman's office. Then it was agreed that we should have a preliminary meeting at Breteuil Avenue in Paris. And there I had my first surprise. I was ushered into a very Spartan office. The shadowy figures that passed by the office now and again glided along noiselessly and unobtrusively in the corridor—the sort of thing you would fully expect the *Red Guide* inspectors to do, who are so important and yet so discreet.[5] Time went by and I waited. There was nothing on the walls to catch a person's eye. They were a neutral, soothing color that reminded me of an old cloister. A door swung open soundlessly.

François Michelin loomed prodigiously near. I had never seen him—not even in photographs, and there I was, quite abashed by the sheer simplicity of the giant. I was struck by his air of authority no less than by his easy good nature.

"Well then," he said to me, "so you want to interview me?"

"Ah . . . yes . . . sure, I would really like to. It is for a morning program on the radio, about six or seven minutes long."

I was all set to give him the names of just a few of the famous people who had been invited to the radio station in the past to participate in this show, when he interrupted me.

"Then, since you want to question me in public, surely you will not mind if I start by interviewing you here, in private?" I agreed to this, of course, and he started:

"Tell me about your life, your childhood, and your plans. What meaning do you give to your life? And tell me right off the bat if you believe in God. If you do not believe in him, tell me why. I would be interested to know the reason. I am keen to talk to people who do not think the way I do. I find that it teaches me a lot of things. Where they draw their strength from. What reality they base their lives on. In fact, for me there is no serious conflict between science and religion, since they both take their point of departure from reality. I would not say the same thing about materialism. I see it as a source of bickering antagonism and strife. Besides, it does not answer the question of what happens after death."

Had he punched me in the stomach, I could not have been more dumbfounded. Never had anything like this happened to me . . . not in my dealings with French or foreign presidents and chairmen, nor with the eccentrics (there are some) to be found in public life or artistic circles. Never had the tables been so utterly turned, transforming the hunted into the hunter in the hidden confines of his own office. And I, to be sure, had the quite rare experience of meeting a gentleman preoccupied with the things of this world and with people but not exclusively so. The element of surprise, moreover, reached a further climax when, at the end of a long, a very long conversation, more philosophical than economic or political, I took my leave of François Michelin, after he had promised to make an appointment with me for a radio broadcast in the following terms:

"Are you in a hurry to interview me? Do you think you are capable of waiting several months or even years?"

"Yes, sir, I am."

As we had talked a great deal about God and a little bit about the ephemeral, fly-by-night nature of the media, I thought, though, that I was entitled to proffer a cautionary remark:

"However, let us be careful, you and I. Imagine if my little morning broadcast were to be canceled and came to an end. Imagine, too, if God called us back to his bosom, you and me, before we had the chance to have our interview. That would be a real shame."

Fifteen years later, in the spring of 1993, François Michelin kept his word and gave an interview on a variety of topics to "The Entrepreneurial Way," a program broadcast on France Inter.[6] This interview attracted a record audience and elicited countless testimonials of approval from the listeners, who appreciated their discovery of a French top executive who spoke with that same air of simplicity and truth that Gaston Bachelard conveys in his writings.[7]

"You were able to wait," he said to me. "You see, patience is always rewarded. I promised you that I would come to explain myself on the radio when I was convinced that it would be worthwhile to make the effort."

Of all the people who hold lofty and important positions in our country, I do not know anyone who would be likely to resist the temptation of an open microphone as he did, even pushing it away and keeping it at arm's length all that long while!

Between François Michelin's promise of an interview and its realization, I had occasion to run into him a few times in the most unlikely places. For example, I ran into him one year, on Bastille Day (July 14), at the Elysèe Palace under François Mitterand, when the parliamentary Right and all the heads of major companies were officially refusing to have anything to do with the invitation extended to them by the head of State. With his typically long strides, François Michelin made his way across the lawn in the full, blazing light of day with scarcely a word about the current state of the economy, as he passed people—people who recognized him and expressed their astonishment at his presence there in whispered tones of surprise.

"I am a citizen of the republic," he exclaimed, "I was invited, and so I came!"

Nor was he at all averse to playing tricks on his CNPF colleagues and irritating them.[8] "As far as we are concerned, you are always rocking the boat, and that gets on our nerves," he was told rather forthrightly by one of them once. A former director of the Bank of France even went so far as to reproach him for looking at problems "from an Auvergne point of view."[9]

What is to be made of the habit he has of telling us he does the dishes at home, that doing the dishes allows him to think about the industrial world? Is this a kind of affectation with François Michelin? I do not think so. We have no reason to doubt his word on this point. It is true. As true as what Antoine Pinay's secretary said to me one day while I was waiting in the reception lounge next to a bowl of fruit:[10]

"Have you seen the price of apples? The president is furious!"

As restrained as it is, Mr. François's anger also has a down-to-earth quality but is mostly directed at the small-minded autocrats who theorize about economics. In every other way, the man is even-tempered, courteous, and respectful of his guests—as, in his turn, Yves Messarovitch can attest to:

My first meeting with François Michelin took place in Clermont-Ferrand four years ago. I had been wanting to see him for a long time but was convinced that a meeting with him would never happen. He was such a reserved individual that it seemed futile from the start even to hope for an interview. As people said at the time, just uttering the name Michelin was already saying too much about him. All the same, I managed to get an appointment with him easily enough. When I arrived at the gate of that old plant on the Place des Carmes,[11] where preparations were under way for a major process of renovation, I was taken to a meeting room furnished with a large, laminated table, about a dozen chairs, an overhead projector, and a white board stuck in the corner on an easel. Adjoining this area, another room contained tires neatly lined up on a metal rack. Michelin tires, of course, but also some of the competition's brand names.

"Ah, you find that interesting?" came the sudden query out of nowhere. It was François Michelin. I had not heard him come in.

"I had never noticed how tread patterns could be so different," I replied to him, as though to excuse myself for having turned my back to him.

"Look here," he explained to me, "on a tire, the groove that drains the water is absolutely essential for safety. This tire here is rather poorly designed, because the water does not drain quickly enough. But then, this is not a Michelin tire!"

That is how we started off our first exchange, which must have lasted a total of four hours—four hours shut up in this room with diffused lighting and no other witnesses, during which time I discovered a man who is totally unlike the image that people commonly have of him: unpretentious, approachable, direct, clear, amusing, and above all, endowed with a wonderful ability to listen. During this four-hour period, which I wanted to be as dense as possible, I decided not to use my tape recorder. I took only some notes by hand, just enough not to put him off, because he was unaccustomed to dealing with any kind of journalist. In my seat on the plane going home, I tried hard to reconstruct, as best I could, the words of the discussion we had had. Then, thanks to another telephone conversation with "Mr. François," I got the go-ahead from him to reproduce his remarks within the framework of a summer miniseries dedicated to "Great and Silent Personalities," which had been requested by my editor, Franz-Olivier Giesbert. That turned out rather well.

Then there was another phone call to François Michelin to get his agreement on the quotes that I could attribute to him. There was no problem on this score, since he is a man who is respectful of other people's work, something that is not, alas, always the rule in interviews. That is how we formed a steady relationship, punctuated by phone calls and meetings here and there. This led, one morning in the beginning of January, to my secretary having the delightful surprise of hearing Mr. Michelin, who was in a very good mood indeed, wish her a "Happy New Year."

Everything about him is distinguished: his bearing, his manner of speech, and his office. This fine figure of a man, tall and elegant, is actually dressed in the most neutral way imaginable: A grayish, nondescript suit, an all-occasion tie, and a solid pair of dress shoes constitute his daily uniform. What a contrast with his thousand-and-one intellectual and spiritual preoccupations! In point of fact, his appearance is merely an outward husk, a social convenience.

As soon as he begins speaking, François Michelin lights up. It should be understood that he does not explain things as one would expect them to be explained in the institutions of higher learning or the universities. His opinions about society, business, politicians, and the great questions of the day are unique. He is the very image of a free man, far removed from the talk that takes place all around him. François Michelin *is* François Michelin. He borrows nothing from the trends of the day. What he is, he owes to his ability to enter into dialogue and to his boundless capacity to remain true to his convictions.

In perfect harmony with himself, he moves about in a universe—his plant, his office—to which no other executive would dare to lay a claim. At home in Clermont-Ferrand, with that smell of rubber that he misses whenever he is away from it, his day begins in the simplest of ways. When he reaches the grounds of the factory at the wheel of his gray BX GTI,[12] he shows his ID badge to the guard, as he does every morning. It makes no difference that he is François Michelin. The rules have to be respected. Then he goes on to park his car a little bit farther ahead on the right. He gets out of the car, unbending his tall frame in an elegant motion that betrays, despite his seventy-two years, a long-standing affinity for the tennis court, tennis being his favorite sport. He walks to a massive wooden door built out of sober oak without any excess of moldings, which leads to the executive offices. Here, there is no receptionist charged with screening the few visitors that would come her way, nor even a waiting room with fancy leather seats. In fact, the executive offices begin in a corridor that has a succession of doors, all alike, on both sides.

On the left, the first one opens up into a small room with yellow walls. A wooden desk, built in the last century at about the same time as the first plant, stands right beside another piece of furniture of undefined style. In a corner, within arm's reach—space is strictly rationed here—there is a shelf that holds a funny-looking model railcar mounted on tires, made from painted food cans—a gift from grateful railway men in Madagascar! This, indeed, is François Michelin's office—monastic: a lamp, three pieces of furniture, and, behind the door, a coatrack with two hooks. Hung carefully from the right-hand hook is a set of overalls.

This office, of extreme modesty, stands in sharp contrast to the economic and financial power it represents. No other enterprise in the world that has sales of more than eighty billion francs would dare to impose such a Spartan regime on its chairman. So François Michelin explains to you, of course, that in order to do good work the important thing is not to be ostentatious. Rather, what is really important is to be found deep within oneself. And he explains that a bare room is more conducive to thought and reflection than a luscious space cluttered up with impressively useless gadgets.

He adds that he is not the only executive in the company, but that the responsibilities are divided up among a handful of men who share the same values in terms of performance, simplicity, and discretion. It has been precisely these three catchwords that have been the guiding light in the education of Edouard Michelin, his thirty-five-year-old son, a graduate of the Ecole Centrale.[13] Edouard recently became managing partner and will take over the helm of succession with his own way of doing things. "He was given the freedom to be himself." Like François, he has learned about life on the job, in the midst of people on the shop floor, to understand them and their jobs better. According to what is said about Edouard by those who have had the chance to work with him, he is endowed with the qualities that are necessary to preside over the destinies of this company, which is more than one hundred years old. For, while Bibendum celebrated his one-hundredth birthday in 1998, the Michelin brand name was born in 1889.[14]

For as long as he has been working with the company, François Michelin has always seen his job as managing partner, as a series of obligations: keeping the vessel on course, protecting passengers and cargo, anticipating events in the world and the conflicting currents of the market but always taking care to satisfy the three groups of people who are entitled, he believes, to hold him accountable: the customers, the employees, and the shareholders.

François Michelin does not establish a hierarchy between those who bring their capital to the enterprise and those who provide it with their work, although he always ranks the customer first. As it was said in the past: The customer is king. The customer is always right. And he is not afraid to add: "It is true. Property is theft, when it is not at the service of people."

Having lunch at the invitation of François Michelin in Clermont or in Paris is a privilege. After all, another one of the hats he wears is as boss of the inspectors for the *Red Guide*, the people who give out stars and forks, and who also withdraw them on occasion. One day, when he had had an enjoyable dinner near the Gare du Nord in Paris, in the company of one of his inspectors, he suggested giving a good grade to the restaurant that they had discovered. "Hold on," the inspector advised, "we should sleep on it." "And he was right, for we were sick during the night," he reports, always quick to salute the practical intelligence and competence of those who work for the company.

He is quick also to rejoice at the virtues of hard work, education, well-understood ethics and morality, an acceptance of and respect for rules, humility, and the acquisition of knowledge through scientific research. He quotes the finely turned phrase of Paul Valèry:[15] "A man who marvels is like a blossoming rose." And François Michelin, distressed by those who confuse causes and effects and state as their first principle the "cogito" of Descartes[16] instead of leaving the matter in the hands of Pascal,[17] smiles as he speaks, beaming with delight.

Obviously, he also has a home in heaven, and this explains his joy and confidence, which does not stop him from digging his furrow, plowing his field, and being an energetic businessman on this earth.

Competence and vision. . . . Thus, Michelin has no great liking for financiers who are only financiers, those who forget the origin of finance and its reality, the theoreticians, the small-minded autocrats of politics, and the government administrations in Paris. "The city mouse rattles off its lessons. . . . The country mouse looks around and sees things." By his speech and his culture, his manners, there is a constant, subtle evocation of the fables of Fontaine or Florian and the dictionaries.[18] If he speaks so clearly, so simply, so vigorously—this person who, ironically, is not heard very much—it is because he has immersed himself in the common language of the workers, because he is a good listener, and because he always goes to check the meaning of his words, not in Larousse or Robert but in Littré.[19]

It is as if he knows that any sort of meaningful exchange is done through language, and that the primary relationship between the worker and his employer happens by way of words. Better make sure, in this case, that the words are well-understood and well-defined from the start.

In this regard, you should hear him touch on the subject of hierarchy: "The boss who is the boss's boss—that pyramidal structure that fouls everything up," as he goes on to state his own preference for a system of free-thinking exchange on the English model. "It is only free thinking," he says, "that is entirely worthy of a free man."

As for the State, which compels and governs rather than opens doors and sets people free, François Michelin does not like it. And here, for example, is what happens if, unfortunately, you should question him about this:

"But in that case why does big business ask the State for so many concessions and so much money?"

His answer is quite plain-spoken and to the point: "Because the State takes it away from us!"

He illustrates his remarks by pointing to the costs inherent to every industrial enterprise that endeavors to raise its productivity: "When you press down a car's gas pedal, you need more gas."

This is the same man who is not afraid to remind his audience, whether they are men from the Left or the Right, about his obsession with rising manpower costs.

"Fifty percent of the wages paid out by Michelin in France are offset by our foreign sales. This need of ours to export in order to survive and remain competitive terrifies me sometimes."

He backs up his pleading for a massive lowering of charges and taxes in France with some figures:

"In our country 100 francs in wages force us to ask for 180 francs from the customer, as compared to less than 130 francs in England. It is this truth, this reality of the market, that weighs so heavily on investment."

And to those who have gone so far as to say, "Michelin is Number One. Michelin is doing all right. Michelin can pay," Mr. François, the third inheritor of the dynasty, paints a picture of the relative extent of his empire with a sigh:

"How can we talk about an empire? We are small in Asia. We enjoy a modest presence in South America, and also we are at the lower limits of what should be done in the United States. If we want to carry on and survive, we have to innovate now, in the future, and also, quite naturally, we have to expand."

Essentially, Michelin sees globalization as being simultaneously both a constraint and a tremendous opportunity. This is the reason why the argument heard in Clermont-Ferrand stresses the damage caused by an overly hasty opening of borders. As early as 1994, François Michelin would explain to his visitors the basic error of GATT (since then, it has become the World Trade Organization): "GATT is like a lock on a canal. Instead of opening the gates gently and slowly, they were raised all at once. The water is surging in. It is not surprising that the barge in the canal is taking a steep plunge."

It would be easy to view this metaphor of the canal lock as an excuse. It would be wrong, however, to make any such hasty judgment. Why, in fact, has Michelin been able to take full advantage of globalization so well? How has a man as reserved as he is succeeded in hoisting his business, in thirty years, from tenth place to first place in the ranks of tire manufacturers?

François Michelin keeps a low profile on this subject. For him, these commercial successes are merely a response—the most appropriate one, no doubt, despite its costs in terms of the suppression of jobs—to the challenges that we are facing. Like a wave that wears away relentlessly at a cliff face, globalization is eating away at French society, forcing it to question itself and disrupting the social relationships in the cities. Clermont-Ferrand, long dubbed "Michelinville" because the company took care of everything for its workers—jobs, schools, hospitals—provides an emblematic illustration of this. Michelin's shareholders, the family being foremost among them, have neither the means nor the political will to keep doing that.

François Michelin has understood this for a long time. He is the one who, having made the decision, convinced his family circle to hasten the advent of change in certain facets of the business, in order to better prepare it for the twenty-first century. In view of the results, this seems to have been the thing to do. Sales of eighty billion francs with four-billion-francs profit in 1997, ultra-

modern plants, loads of plans and projects: All the ingredients of a lasting success seem to have come together now, but this sort of conclusion makes François
Michelin jump because he knows that these achievements can very quickly turn
into an illusion, because every day he experiences the menacing onslaughts of
advancing competition. The fault, as he explains in this book, lies not in globalization itself—whether one is for or against it is not the real debate, seeing that it
is an inescapable fact—but in the politicians who have dominated the scene in
France for several generations. France has been governed by the spiritual sons of
Marx. And for what result? Prohibitive manpower costs keep going up, precisely
when it is the opposite that should be happening.

Competition should prompt our government to implement the means by
which these costs might be brought down in order to combat—as François
Michelin does it—the transfer of plants to foreign countries and to save jobs.
Today the heart of Michelin is the world, but the soul of its helmsman continues
to reside at the foot of the Puy de Dôme, where his family took its rise and where
it will continue to live for a long time yet.

In brief, therefore, these conversations constitute a testimony. They express
the muted, sometimes fierce, anger of an authentic, sincere man who is also a
nonconformist, whose immense charismatic aura is inversely proportional to his
public appearances. Over twenty years, these public appearances can, in fact, be
counted on the fingers of one hand. We, ourselves, who have rubbed shoulders
with him throughout this interview process, do not claim to have penetrated all
the secrets of one of the most celebrated top executives in France.

There is a bit of Jules Verne in this man.[20] His ability to see into the future,
to imagine new machines, and to use simple language to express complex ideas
might have made him a successful writer. There are few people, in fact, who are
as good at using vivid images and parables to convince others of the legitimacy
of their intuitions. "If I use simple words when I speak, my intent quite simply is
to be sure that I understand what I am saying," he says in his defense, not without a touch of disarming humor. The fact remains that behind the barely masked
nostalgia for a vanished world, Clermont's industrialist has already stepped foot
into the twenty-first century. The succession has been settled. The business has a
presence in 170 countries, and new manufacturing processes—the details are
confidential—have burst onto the scene. They should give Michelin a serious
jump on its competitors, starting with the already famous "C3M" machine, to
which the press has made allusions on several occasions and which is going to
revolutionize methods of production.

Michelin the innovator also radiates a great deal of that quiet joy that can be
found in the prewar films of Julien Duvivier.[21] This man accepts the rules of
mass production and the wide distribution of standardized goods, but he has not
given up on the old-fashioned notion of good, sound work reminiscent of the
trade guilds.

François Michelin is a man who is always grumbling about the decline of France, a country where, since 1936,[22] all the governments have placed such heavy burdens on the donkey, that they have made the animal falter and stumble. One day they may even work it into the ground. This same François Michelin strongly condemns the thirty-five-hour workweek, as plants in the United States run 350 days a year compared to 280 days in France. François Michelin regards Marx and his heirs as partisans of an economy controlled, planned, and administered by the State, as those who are most responsible for France's misfortunes. Nevertheless, he maintains an enthusiastic outlook about mankind in general. It is the structures generating irresponsibility that he is against, with the collusions that they foster between different powers and the bureaucracy that battens on them. This is not something that he does as humanity's benefactor but as a man of goodwill who recognizes the importance of concrete realities. It is in this sense that François Michelin comes across these days as "the last of the Mohicans." Industrialist, wealthy Christian capitalist, both philosopher and worker, anonymous and well-known, he is the only living Frenchman whose name is inseparable from a commodity product that has an international reputation, one that has left its impression on the roadways of the world with tracks that are, at the same time, deep-set and faint.

—Ivan Levaï and Yves Messarovitch

Notes and Explanations

1. Puy-Guillaume: Small town twenty-five miles outside of Clermont-Ferrand.
2. Puy de Dôme: One of the mountains ten miles from Clermont-Ferrand; altitude 4,900 ft.; gave its name to the whole administrative region.
3. Jacques Tati (1908–1982): French filmmaker famous for his often silent and meditating character, Mr. Hulot.
4. *Le Figaro*: Famous French newspaper; positioned center-center right.
5. *Red Guide*: Published in 1900 by Michelin; restaurant and hotel guide that refers the famous "stars" every year to the best restaurants.
6. France Inter: One of the most listened-to, State-owned radio channels.
7. Gaston Bachelard (1884–1962): French philosopher.
8. CNPF: Conseil National du Patronat Français; association of French employers created in 1946.
9. Auvergne: Name of the region in the center of France whose capital city is Clermont-Ferrand.
10. Antoine Pinay (1891–1994): French politician, several times minister under the Fourth Republic; famous for his good, down-to-earth common sense; last finance minister under General Charles de Gaulle.
11. Place des Carmes: In Clermont-Ferrand; main square where the Michelin headquarters are located.

François Michelin—A Gentleman

12. BX GTI: Medium-size Citroen automobile.
13. Ecole Centrale: Ecole Centrale des Arts et Manufactures; one of the three or four top engineering schools in Paris.
14. Bibendum: Name of the "Michelin man." In 2000, Bibendum was voted the best-known logo in the world.
15. Paul Valèry (1871–1945): French poet and writer.
16. René Descartes (1596–1650): French mathematician and philosopher; author of *Discourse on the Method of Properly Guiding the Reason in the Search of Truth in the Sciences.*
17. Blaise Pascal (1623–1662): Born in Clermont-Ferrand. Philosopher and physicist; invented the calculating machine.
18. Jean La Fontaine (1621–1695): Poet, famous for his fables; Jean Pierre de Florian (1755–1794): wrote five books of fables.
19. Larousse and Littré: Names of two very much-used French dictionaries; Larousse being more-everyday explanations and Littré being more into semantics and etymology.
20. Jules Verne (1828–1905): French writer famous for, among others, *Twenty Thousand Leagues Under the Sea* and *Around the World in Eighty Days.*
21. Julien Duvivier (1896–1967): French moviemaker.
22. The year 1936—Year of the Popular Front: Generated by the alliance of Socialists and Marxist parties within the national assembly marked by sweeping nationalizations.

PREFACE

Why a Dialogue?

Reality is a harsh, uncompromising teacher. I say "teacher" because it is always unceremoniously exploding ready-made ideas and prejudices. How does reality manifest itself?—almost always through men and women who are busy at their work. It is they who teach us and nurture us in one form or another in the fascinating diversity of their real-life responsibilities.

The responsibilities that I have assumed over the last forty-seven years have led me to seek answers from the people working with me, to the questions that come my way. This relationship with concrete, everyday realities contributes something essential to life, as it forces people to make hard, binding decisions that they have to live with.

Also, there are particular moments that in our "shoptalk" we call "question-and-answer sessions." These take place one-on-one or in groups of various sizes and importance and, during them, any question whatsoever can be asked, even one that runs like this: "How do you reconcile the fact that you are a business executive, with your Catholic faith?" This is a question that I, for my part, reformulate in the following way: "Is there such a thing as a human experience of the business world?" Actually, in the everyday reality of life, every person stands revealed as a free creation. This is why everyone is unique. All of life's successes and failures are the means by which this free creation seeks to forge its way in the bustling world of men, in a scientific, technical world. . . . In the business world, as well, it is essential that this free creation somehow not lose sight of the essence of its own mode of functioning. This free creation must not be made to feel that it is caught up in something that it has come to regard as a blind determinism.

Freedom, technology, ethics: Questions touching on these topics were also raised several times by Messrs. Levaï and Messarovitch, with whom I have had the pleasure of engaging in an exchange of ideas. They, too, acknowledged the importance of concrete reality and have seen fit to express themselves by drawing on a different range of sensibilities, experiences, and occupations. The questions to which both of them are seeking answers are the same questions that I am asking myself, too. This is how the idea was conceived that we should join forces and try to arrive at answers to all these questions together. The resulting dialogue has allowed me to learn a great deal and to see problems in what is, for me, a fresh, new light. My answers are an endeavor to appeal to freedom of conscience and opinion.

The main thing is to live, but in order to do this, one has to feed on the reality that is hidden behind facts, one has to seek out root causes. To have a respectful attitude, a person has to take into account facts, not opinions, be it in the realm of religion, philosophy, or, on a more mundane level, politics. What really counts, what remains important in the final analysis is lived reality, not the "external characteristics" of the person who is doing the talking. This makes every human interaction a fulfilling experience. It allows us to build freedom.

On no account is this book meant to be construed as a judgment on any person. I know the extent to which all the good intentions in the world are apt to be revealed as inadequate when it comes to the actual real-life achievement.

The experience that the three of us have lived together in order to write this book will serve to demonstrate, I think, how the sharing of a certain attitude of mind and heart can be a mainspring of progress. When one agrees, without preconceived ideas, to go in search of the reality that defines people and things, this reality does not let itself be tied into any ideological framework.

It is the earnest wish of all three of us that the mystery that exists in every man and every woman should be recognized and acknowledged. May this acknowledgment polish and refine our outlook on life and our ability to listen, becoming the foundation of all our actions.

And why not . . .?

—François Michelin

1

The Factory

IVAN LEVAÏ: When we broached the idea of a title for this work, what came to your mind was "What the 'Factory' Taught Me." You used the word *factory*. Why didn't you refer to "the company"?

FRANÇOIS MICHELIN: *Company* is a word that is currently very much in style, but so vague that it is getting hard to know what is implied by it. Also, it is somewhat nondescript. *Factory*, on the other hand, conjures up notions of machines, things that are produced, and, most important, men and women who are employees, customers, and shareholders.

I have often asked people outside our company, who, they thought, was the most important individual in it. Their answers take on the coloring of their respective political or social opinions. For some, it is the employer; for others, it is the union leader or the workers or the supervisor, or occasionally the controller or sales manager. "You are mistaken," I say to them. "The most important individual is the customer." Their reply is that the customer is not a part of the business. "But when I have a large stock of tires sitting in the warehouse, what can I do? How do I pay wages?" I reply. When a product is manufactured, whether it be tires or tape recorders, wealth is only created once they are sold. The customer is not only an integral part of the company, but he enjoys a fantastic transcendent relationship to it because he can remain faithful to it or, on the contrary, take his business elsewhere whenever he wants. The customer is nothing like the captive audience that the taxpayer is. I feel like saying that the company is like a verb whose subject is the customer.

1

IVAN LEVAÏ: But the customer is an outsider to the business. He never goes there. He stays at a distance. You cannot put a face on him.

FRANÇOIS MICHELIN: Every customer is a distinct individual. Automobile manufacturers play an important part in our sales, and, believe me, we know the faces of the people who buy our tires quite well. One must never lose sight of the fact that the customer is the beginning and the end of everything.

YVES MESSAROVITCH: Is not the term *factory* somewhat outdated? Do not people say they are going to work at a certain company rather than "at such and such factory"? Even the expression "factory work" seems utterly outdated.

FRANÇOIS MICHELIN: And yet, "factory work" expresses perfectly what we do every day. Essentially, it is an action that consists of taking raw materials and making a marketable product out of them. It is a noble act. To engage in factory work, you have to have an in-depth knowledge of the kind of materials that you are working with. You have to have a love for these materials—in the strongest sense of the word *love*—you have to like them just the way they are.

IVAN LEVAÏ: Even in the case of rubber, which has such an awful smell?

FRANÇOIS MICHELIN: It is amazing to see how tires, for many people, are something round, black, and dirty, with an awful smell. I can assure you that nobody in the company looks at them this way!

YVES MESSAROVITCH: They are also an instrument for play and leisure, since they allow a person to travel, to go on vacation, or to leave for the weekend.

FRANÇOIS MICHELIN: You mean—the automobile. It is also an excellent tool. The automobile is the modern-day equivalent of the horse. The French are not at all mistaken in their views on it. When they are asked what, in their estimation, has been the most important invention of the century, 51 percent of them answer: "The automobile."

YVES MESSAROVITCH: Did your ancestors have some inkling of this phenomenon? How did the Michelins come to have an interest in tires? Did they have a sense in their own time of the economic stakes that were involved with the coming of the automobile and the implications arising from both its military and civilian uses?

FRANÇOIS MICHELIN: Everything started with the arrival of an English cyclist in our plant yard. His bicycle had been loaded onto an oxcart because one of his tires had been punctured. He had come to Clermont-Ferrand where, he had been told, there was a rubber plant. His bicycle tire had been developed by a certain Mr. Dunlop, a veterinarian by profession, who was fed up with traveling the country roads on a bike with wheels that were only simple iron rims covered with a strip of rubber. One day Mr. Dunlop had the marvelous idea of putting a cushion of air between the wheel and the ground so as to enhance his comfort while cycling. *He was the real inventor of the tire.*

But let us go back a bit further. The firm had been founded in 1832 by two partners, Aristide Barbier and Nicolas Edouard Daubrèe. Mr. Daubrèe had married the niece of a Scottish chemical engineer (Macintosh), who had discovered the process that allowed rubber to dissolve and be made into a sort of glue that was used to manufacture raincoats. When the Daubrèe family settled in Clermont-Ferrand, Mrs. Daubrèe brought rubber with her.

Aristide Barbier's daughter married Jules Michelin, a customs officer at Limoges at a time when that city exported its china and earthenware worldwide.[1] Jules Michelin was a respectable employee of the public treasury but also had a remarkable talent for etching. In his youth, in fact, he had painted with Gros.[2] Jules had three children: Marie, Andrè, and Edouard, who was my grandfather.

When these children became adults, the family business was in a shambles, nearly collapsing. Having finished his studies at Ecole Centrale, Andrè went to Clermont-Ferrand and ten days later returned home, discouraged and convinced that nothing more could be done to save the company.

Edouard, who had taken law and studied painting with Bouguereau,[3] decided to go there to check things out as well. When he arrived at the plant, he saw two workers busily boiling a treetop of sorb wood in a bucket. As you know, the sorb tree is well known for the density and hardness of its wood. Surprised, he approached them and asked them what they were doing. They answered him: "Make sure that you do not tell the boss. He does not want us going in the garden. But, you know, gear cogs are so expensive in town that we have to make do on our own somehow." My grandfather always told me that he came to understand what was at the core of doing business when he witnessed this human power and energy at work, this desire to make progress, this sense of economy and thrift. He stayed in Clermont-Ferrand. Everyone thought that he was mad, but for him it was both an exciting discovery and a duty.

He invented all kinds of things. At the time, carriages had brake blocks that made a horrific noise, something like the sound the trolley cars make in Strasbourg when they are heading into a turn![4] They made an awful, squealing noise. Grandfather perfected a brake block that made no noise: "THE SILENT."

And then the English cyclist arrived. Grandfather made the repair in two hours. He got on the bike and took a ride around the yard. The tire immediately got another flat. *This would be a great invention*, he thought to himself, *but only if the tire could be fixed in fewer than ten minutes.* Six months later, the tire that can be disassembled was invented. To prove its effectiveness, a bicycle race was organized in Clermont-Ferrand. Andrè Michelin had the terrific idea of going to the hardware store to buy nails that could stay pointed up in the air. He laid them all along the cycling route. Everyone got a flat tire, but the cyclists on the Michelin team were back in the saddle within minutes. As for the others, it took them two hours to make their repairs.

It is this story that makes me say that, in business, the customer is the beginning and the end of everything. This idea is deeply programmed into the "genes" of the company. What does the customer want? What is he saying? How can we improve things for him?

YVES MESSAROVITCH: You say that the customer is the beginning and the end of everything, but he is quite passive as compared to the hardworking innovators who are forever demonstrating a freshly original and vital spirit of creativity.

FRANÇOIS MICHELIN: I do not agree. When a person spends money, he is totally involved in his purchase. He is making a choice between different desires, different products. It is an irreversible choice. Of course, in certain instances, if you are not happy, you get your money back. But this is not something you can do with every product you buy—with a car, for example, it is impossible. The act of purchasing is a free and responsible action, one that involves the whole personality. It is an eminently formative act.

It is formative for the person who is purchasing, and formative for the vendor. Take a pin. It is absolutely phenomenal when you realize everything that was necessary in order to manufacture it: iron ore, coal, enormous smelting furnaces—not to mention an extraordinarily elaborate effort of the imagination—and all the careful work that goes into its making. All this effort and energy to arrive at this little trifling thing, only just so big!

IVAN LEVAÏ: Over the course of a century some of this has been forgotten.

FRANÇOIS MICHELIN: Yes, some of it, but there is much that still remains. Just look at the pride you can find among the workers in the plants. It is impressive and so human.

YVES MESSAROVITCH: Industrial products have never been as sophisticated as they are today. All the same, the act of purchasing has become utterly insignificant. In the past, buying tires or a tape recorder represented a serious outlay of money. Nowadays, the amount of money set aside for these things is less than what you would spend to go on vacation or to go to the doctor. How do you explain this insignificance?

FRANÇOIS MICHELIN: Insignificance means *has become commonplace*. As far as I am concerned, that is great! It does not necessarily mean that there is a drop in quality. It is the concept of mass production, driven by the market economy that has allowed this. Unfortunately, the climate that surrounds this economic reality is pernicious, and this is what clouds the issue. This is Marx's fault. By artificially stressing the fundamental opposition between producers and consumers, by arguing that one is stealing from the other, he completely overshadowed the human factor in the relationship, which binds men to one another by way of work and money. Thus, he turned an act of service into grounds for conflict and stripped it of its meaning. This is what started State planning.

Like a number of philosophers of his time, Marx mistook consequences for causes. He tells, for example, how struck he was when he noticed that financiers and industrialists always had the word *capital* on their lips. But what do you expect? The main concern of the captain of a ship is the hull of his boat, and that is what he talks about before he gets around to talking about the rest of it. If there is a hole in the hull, the boat sinks.

YVES MESSAROVITCH: For Marx, the exchange that takes place is marked by conflict. For you, the exchange is one of complicity. The buyer and the vendor are on the same boat, and the exchange is in some way or other even and equal. There are theories, however, that speak of an uneven, unequal exchange.

FRANÇOIS MICHELIN: You need a tire. As for me, I need to pay wages and my shareholders. The money I receive serves many purposes.

If you look beyond the short term of human life, the act of exchange is a process that is fundamental for the producer and the buyer. The market economy is the only one that works, because it truly brings men into a relationship with one another. And, personally, I prefer to speak of "the economy of responsible choice" rather than the market economy, for the market is simply the place where choices are made.

IVAN LEVAÏ: You accuse Marx of having polluted economic life with his theory of class struggle, but is not Taylor a major culprit?[5] Have not the main principles that he established overshadowed creativity, and the "nice piece of handicraft" that people went into raptures about in the past?

FRANÇOIS MICHELIN: Taylor's method consisted of making an inventory of useful and useless operations. His first study dealt with the problems of a steelmaking factory that was having trouble keeping its furnaces stoked properly. Taylor realized that the workers had been given huge shovels. This meant that every ten minutes they were forced to stop and catch their breath. He showed that, by using smaller shovels and having more people working, it was possible to increase the output significantly.

Very often it is only Taylor's concept of breaking down tasks into individual operations that people remember, and people remember it only to denounce it, of course. It has been forgotten that more than anything else this was a response to the growing complexity of manufactured items at the beginning of large companies, when men and women did not have the necessary level of training. You had to put, to work, people who had not been trained at all. Breaking down tasks into individual operations allowed them to learn a job quickly. His method allowed industry to get off the ground, enabling many people to be better served with some "nice pieces of handicraft."

The most common error stems from judging things from the outside and not on the inside. Taylor's analyses were consistent with a superior level of coherence.

If you go see the sewers of Paris, you are going to say to yourself: *This is outrageous, disgusting; how can people be made to work in there?* The only conclusion then that should be drawn from such an attitude is that people should no longer eat or wash! In life there are, inevitably, dull and dusty things. To take these things for granted is to forget that often they are, in fact, only consequences of something that is infinitely superior to them.

YVES MESSAROVITCH: In your opinion, therefore, the whole thing is a seamless whole. It means that the product itself cannot be dissociated from becoming commonplace in the eyes of the customer and the methods of production that have been implemented to make it.

FRANÇOIS MICHELIN: This exists more in our minds than is the case in reality. If you go to a Home Center, you will see the care with which buyers choose objects as insignificant as nails. Their choosing cannot by any means be said to be "insignificant." When you buy shoes, even though this is not a significant purchase, all the same, you devote a half hour, sometimes even three-quarters of an hour, to choosing your shoes because you do not want shoes that will make your feet sore.

IVAN LEVAÏ: You say, "In life there are, inevitably, dull and dusty things." This is a very nice expression, but isn't it the same people who are always being saddled with the inevitably dull and dusty things? What do you think about the evolution of the working class?

FRANÇOIS MICHELIN: I remember a plant worker who was clearly capable of becoming a supervisor. I suggested it to him. To my surprise, he replied: "Mr. Michelin, you are very kind, but the plant is not the main focus of my interests. Do not ask me to get more involved in it than I already am." I found this answer inherently respectable. There are people who have a passion for their job. There are others, however, whose interests are focused elsewhere. It is obvious that they aspire to develop their talents, to become what they potentially are, but outside the plant. It is very difficult to arrive at a proper judgment about any given state of affairs without listening to the person and his deepest motivations. If you lose sight of this, you are losing sight of an essential aspect of the problem.

One day, someone approached me in the plant: "Mr. François, how do you explain the infighting between departments?" I replied, "When you jump out of bed in the morning, don't you ever ask yourself questions? Isn't there something in your mind that prompts you to ask yourself why you are getting up and whether you should get going or not? Deep within you, you are always in the state of choosing. Deep within each of us, there is division. This is also an expression of our freedom. Why should things be different between departments, seeing as they are made up of people who have the same characteristics as you do?"

To tackle the problem of conflict between departments by putting in place a structure that tries to make them work together is to work on the consequences, not on the cause. On the other hand, to ponder the question of what should be done to take men and women where they are and train them in such a way that they come to an understanding of the general problems that face the company as well as the relationships and interactions within, is to engage in a wonderful task. You create a team, with an atmosphere of respect for different personalities. I admit that this is easy to say but quite difficult to do in practice, precisely because deep within ourselves we are all divided.

IVAN LEVAÏ: You are always coming back to people—from the company to people.

FRANÇOIS MICHELIN: And to people as a customer. Fundamentally, "the economy of responsible choice" possesses an utterly essential dimension for one's growth. That is why there has to be respect for a code of ethics. A person has no right to lie. When you say something untrue to someone, it is as if you were handing a child a can of food that has gone bad. And if you are not always asking yourself if what you are doing is good, you slip!

IVAN LEVAÏ: You say that a person has no right to lie. But does he have the right to seduce people? In a way, those who produce have to seduce people.

FRANÇOIS MICHELIN: You can seduce someone by "polluting" his judgment. This does not last. Or else, you can confront the person with real problems that he has to resolve. Every object is a compromise. Take a professional photographer's camera and a disposable camera. Buying one or the other of these has to do with a choice that involves a compromise. Everything depends on what you want to do with it. Basically, truth is the only real form of seduction, when you get right down to it.

YVES MESSAROVITCH: With the technological progress that has been made, the difference in quality has become less of a factor. The quality of disposable cameras is almost the same as that of the reflex cameras of a few years ago. Quality has become a banal consideration, has it not?

FRANÇOIS MICHELIN: Once again, let us be careful about the word *banal*. It has become extremely pejorative. Nevertheless, it has very interesting connotations. In old English, the "banal" oven is the oven that is set up for everybody's use. In point of fact, the word *banal* is eminently democratic. Nowadays more and more people have access to high-quality products at more reasonable prices. In the area of cars, take the Twingo, for instance.[6] It goes as fast as the prewar Citroïn. This is phenomenal.

I might add that the search for quality in every sphere of business activity is also an extraordinary unifying agent that brings the people in the company together. It is especially through this never-ending search for higher quality in terms of products and services that our personal relationship with our customers is made manifest to everybody in the company. It is expressed through a continuous effort to improve the level of performance, to guarantee the consistency of products and services, and to cut down on our costs. Every detail counts. The passion for innovation and quality is the very lifeblood of business.

IVAN LEVAÏ: When people are prompted to buy a VCR, they are handed a device that could almost be used as equipment for a professional video technician. Many people use only one or two of the six or seven functions that are available to them. In a way, haven't they been somewhat cheated?

FRANÇOIS MICHELIN: I would not say that. Deep down, the buyers were hoping to do something with this or that function, but they realize that they do not need it. That is all right, but for them the important thing, when all is said and done, is to have that capability when they want it. You know, there are many people who are happy to own a car, even if it stays in their garage almost all year round. The fact that they know that they can use it on any given day is enough to satisfy them.

YVES MESSAROVITCH: It is a kind of virtual wealth.

IVAN LEVAÏ: Or a polluting seduction.

FRANÇOIS MICHELIN: It is a degree of potential freedom that makes for dreams. Man has the need to "embark on a journey around his room," as Xavier de Maistre put it.[7]

IVAN LEVAÏ: For you, in the end, the word *banal* really means "something that is of benefit to everybody"?

FRANÇOIS MICHELIN: Yes, something that is available to everyone and allows everybody to live better. With less money.

IVAN LEVAÏ: In short, as an industrialist, you consider yourself to be at the source of our happiness. Aren't you also responsible for our misfortunes? To make roads—trees, and, indeed, whole forests have been cut down; everything was then paved over. And, in the final analysis, people are crammed into cities where you cannot even drive anymore. You have opened up horizons for us, but at the end of it all, it feels as if we have hit a brick wall. When it comes down to it, you are guilty.

FRANÇOIS MICHELIN: No. I do not think that an industrialist can think that he is at the source of other people's happiness, for happiness belongs to a different order of things, as does misfortune, too. But your query poses the obvious question of responsibility. Every action has its consequences. The problem is that if you take negative consequences as being certain when they are still only hypothetical, you are paralyzed and no longer dare take action. You have to accept the dust on the road. It is true that trees have been cut to make highways, but don't newspapers also need wood pulp to make paper? The problem is, making sure that people can meet one another and interact. It is the same with the Internet. It can be extremely polluting and, at the same time, it has the potential to be extremely beneficial. All of this is merely an expression of the responsibility that we have to exercise our freedom in what we do and what we are. What seems to me to be the most important aspect of the human being is that he is self-teachable. Education presupposes that a person should always keep in mind the relationship between an action and its consequences. As I understand it, the essential strength that underlies "the economy of choice," its specifically human dimension, is that it allows every person to measure the consequences of his or her actions. When a painter has an exhibition, it is because he wants to know how he rates as an artist, what people think of him and his work. When the company's salesmen go to visit a tire dealer, they take note of how people perceive us and what improvements we need to make. What about the media too? They spend their time monitoring how they stand in the ratings to find out if the "customer" is satisfied with what he has seen or heard. They are merely weighing the consequences of their actions.

YVES MESSAROVITCH: If we extrapolate from your argument and look at Michelin, which has spanned the century and which represents the ideal synthesis of everything we have known over the last hundred years, your positive contributions over this time period are quite evident. Also evident are the limits of what you have introduced, things from which we have all profited with a highly passive sort of complicity. What about the next stage? In your mind, what are the consequences of all this? The wheel turns, but where is it going to take us?

FRANÇOIS MICHELIN: We do not make tires, but objects that can be of help in transporting people who need to travel, as cheaply and as safely as possible while taking into account the existing technological means. The day that we forget that we are manufacturing things that are oriented toward service as their end, is the day that we will be making a possibly fatal mistake.

YVES MESSAROVITCH: So, then, people do not make an adequate assessment of causes and their consequences. Somewhere you refuse to take into account the implicit consequences of what you do.

FRANÇOIS MICHELIN: Not at all! Why so much anxiety? What did the Romans do? They cut down forests in order to construct their Roman roads. The rabbits in the forest make their little trails. Dogs mark out their territory in their own way. And the world does not stop turning because of this—on the contrary! We, too, are making our own path. Where will we be in twenty or thirty years?—maybe in a less polluted world, after all. Nuclear fusion will make it possible to produce electricity very cheaply. All the thermal power stations that run on oil or coal will disappear. Twenty years from now, we will be driving cars that run on hydrogen. In short, there will be substantially less pollution.

YVES MESSAROVITCH: But when it comes down to it, whatever we produce in this life—whether it be tires or some other thing—what gives us the right to ignore a part of the consequences of our actions and imagine that it is no longer our problem?

FRANÇOIS MICHELIN: But, of course, it *is* our problem! It is a reason for us to do more.

Nevertheless, a person never really knows the complete consequences of his actions. When you throw a pebble into the Seine,[8] you may be disturbing a salmon in Newfoundland and yet not know it. Consequently, what you have to do is to take the utmost precautions. Take, for example, an aspirin tablet. If it had been known beforehand what a great number of stomach perforations it would cause, it would never have been put on the market. All the same, in other respects it is a marvelous product. We live our lives in ignorance.

I do not want to be misunderstood here. People are always saying that they are entitled to make a mistake. This does not mean that they are entitled to make mistakes intentionally. But you have to know how to take risks. A person is duty-bound to conduct experiments, even while being especially attentive to their long-term consequences. It is the basic act that governs innovation. To achieve this, past experiences can light the way, but there comes a time when uncertainty enters into play. If you do not make use of it to try things out, to make daring experiments, you are making a mistake.

YVES MESSAROVITCH: So it is this mysterious area of uncertainty that draws our imagination and encourages us to make progress. Oscar Wilde said that "Progress is simply the expression of utopia." Is it not also a notion that is the expression of mystery?

FRANÇOIS MICHELIN: The economy of responsible choice rests on an element of mystery and risk. The vendor is always being confronted with fresh, new enigmas. I remember being in a store one day and wanting to buy a record player. I looked at the bottom-of-the-line products, and then I looked a bit farther up, then farther still, and gradually I realized that I had been drawn to products that were more and more expensive. Finally, I left without buying anything. The things that I really liked were unreasonably costly. As I left, the owner, who was puzzled, asked me: "What should I do? Should I open one, separate store for my top-of-the-line products, another store for my middle-of-the-line things, and yet a third store for the bottom of the line?" Neither of us had an answer to this question.

IVAN LEVAÏ: Basically, the good fortunes of Michelin rest on the wheel, which is altogether the most extraordinary and the simplest of inventions.

FRANÇOIS MICHELIN: Very much so. When it was fastened onto a wheel, the tire became of service to the car. It is a simple extension of a simple invention. Things always begin by being complicated. Then, as you make the effort to try to understand them, they become simpler.

IVAN LEVAÏ: All the same, it is the radial tire that is your claim to fame.

FRANÇOIS MICHELIN: The radial tire was born out of the difficulties experienced with the standard tire. The standard tire could not go more than eighty miles an hour without blowing up. We had to find a tire that did not heat up as much. Marius Mignol, the researcher who discovered it, had joined the company as a worker in our printing department. He ended up becoming the tire engineer of the century.

IVAN LEVAÏ: Without the benefit of an education, Marius Mignol fulfilled himself at Michelin.

FRANÇOIS MICHELIN: Totally. He was also an outstanding mineralogist who could talk to you about anything. He is the one who explained atomic science to me. You know, some people recruit their inventors from lofty mountain heights, but sometimes it is the ignorant person who has the advantage over someone who has learned, in that he does not live in a graveyard of ideas.

YVES MESSAROVITCH: Do you know that phrase from Montesquieu:[9] "I like peasants because they are not learned enough to make mistakes"?

FRANÇOIS MICHELIN: It is essential to be able to say: "I do not know." This is precisely the attitude of the truly learned man, who is always launching out into areas that are beyond the limits of his knowledge.

YVES MESSAROVITCH: Do you believe in the influence of luck with regard to inventions?

FRANÇOIS MICHELIN: Personally, I do not believe in luck at all. It does not exist. There are people who know how to see, and others who will never see anything. Take Sir Alexander Fleming, for instance, who, as a doctor during World War I, saw otherwise healthy people dying. He realized that he had to find a way to kill the microbes that were festering in their wounds. He already had the notion of antibiotics in mind. One day he noticed that a staphylococcus culture had been stopped by a kind of mold: *Penicillium notatum*. He had discovered penicillin. All around us, the world is full of things that can nourish our freedom. All you have to do is be attentive enough to discover them.

And innovation also demands a boldness and daring. Let me tell you an anecdote that I am quite fond of. Before the war, when Michelin was interested in railway transportation with a view to outfitting some trains with tires, the whole problem boiled down to making the railcars, which were to become known as "Michelines," light enough to render them compatible with the load-carrying capacities of the tires of the time. Drawing their inspiration from aeronautical design, the technical teams devised an aluminum structure that was so light and pliable that the "belly" of the prototype sagged onto the rails. Summoned before Edouard Michelin, and rather ill at ease, they were surprised to find themselves being congratulated for having dared to go to the limits of the experiment. In fact, a few properly placed, steel tie-rods proved to be enough to make this invention viable. Thus, it was made possible for the revolutionary concept of the "rail-tire" to emerge. Did you know that there is a Micheline still in service in Madagascar?

This is the sort of attitude that explains why innovation has remained at the heart of our company. It frees the imagination and encourages risk taking—going to the limits in order to see what happens.

IVAN LEVAÏ: A business dies when the thing it makes is no longer useful or has been replaced by something else. We have seen whole corporations disappear. What would the end of tires be like?

FRANÇOIS MICHELIN: The first question that we have to ask ourselves is the following: We must ascertain whether, after taking into account the specific nature of our business, there will always be transportation in either public or private form. Is transportation a fundamental given or a passing phenomenon of life in society? The answer strikes me as being self-evident. If we do not want to have megalopolistic cities, but human-size cities, then we have to have both public and private means of transportation to link them up together.

There is a second question that we must ask ourselves. We have to ascertain what sorts of means of transportation will be used in the future. Today we have bicycles, scooters, motorcycles, cars, trains, buses, et cetera. Is it possible to imagine something that would replace these means? As things stand now, it is hard to envision anything. Thirty-five years ago we asked ourselves about the nature of the force that made the moon circle the earth. Was it not possible to harness this force and use it for transportation? We have not yet found any way of doing so, although this is not to say that one day something may be found. We have also studied the air cushion as a potential solution to this problem—but seeing that it takes two-hundred-fifty-horsepower motors to lift three people, I do not think that this is the answer.

Every six months we ask ourselves questions like these, in order to assess the danger of us disappearing one day. And then we end up being reassured, when we assess the full extent of the advantages of the wheel. The reality is that it allows us to travel—over any terrain—something that is absolutely exceptional!

What about the tire? Could it be replaced one day? You would have to find a like sort of product, one with the same qualities. What are these qualities? It carries a load, allows a vehicle to accelerate and to brake, and to turn left or right, is noiseless, does not use up energy, is not expensive and, if at all possible, it ought to look good. Its basic function consists of absorbing the irregularities of the ground by using the least costly and lightest "spring" possible: namely, air. A pneumatic tire is the envelope or casing into which is blown *pneuma*,[10] which is none other than breath or air. What could you replace this with? Some ideas are under investigation, but, when it comes to such alternative means, the stumbling blocks are always questions of weight and price of the spring.

Given the state of our present-day knowledge, the tire still has a long life ahead of it.

YVES MESSAROVITCH: Could you tell us some more about any leads that you may have in terms of substitutes that you can imagine for the tire?

FRANÇOIS MICHELIN: We try to imagine such substitutes, but there are always difficulties that prove to be a stumbling block.

YVES MESSAROVITCH: Are they technical or conceptual?

FRANÇOIS MICHELIN: Both. Through observation we are confronted with a number of mysteries that we try to understand. Behold a skier who is coming down a slope. Above his hips, his body remains practically immobile. His knees, on the other hand, bend and straighten at full speed. At what moment does bone become tendon? And when does tendon become muscle? The question can also be asked as to why there is no wheel in nature. Why doesn't man have wheels rather than feet? Or else you can ponder the mystery of the camel's feet! How can a camel walk through sand and stones without injury? What is there about the camel's foot that could be applied to the tire?

IVAN LEVAÏ: You make tires that are of an extraordinarily high quality now, subject to fewer and fewer flats. But among the features of the tire that you just mentioned, there is one that remains highly significant, both for the company and the people who work in it, not to mention the shareholders: You have to *replace* it! What would happen if, in one fell swoop, technological progress made it possible for the customer, once he had bought a car and tires, never to have to change them?

FRANÇOIS MICHELIN: You do not have to be Malthusian![11] The radial tire gives you three times more mileage than the conventional tire. Well, we brought it out in spite of the prophets of doom who tried to talk us out of it even within the company itself. According to them, production was going to drop by two-thirds. The tire dealers would be furious. For every three tires, they would be selling just one. Not only that, but the whole thing was going to be costly since there would have to be investment in new machines, and people would have to be trained. The boss at the time, Mr. Puiseux, decided to test the tire on a stretch of road that he knew well, between Clermont-Ferrand and the Jura Mountains.[12] In doing so, he realized that it was taking him half an hour less time to make the same trip, that he was less tired, that he was using less gas, and that he could cover this distance more pleasantly. All of this was good for the customer. So, there were no two ways about it: We had to bring out the radial tire.

YVES MESSAROVITCH: When some of the management staff are opposed to a project, who makes the decision?

FRANÇOIS MICHELIN: The boss. He is the only one who can commit the company at this point. The risk involved was an important consideration, of course, but had we declined to bring out the radial tire, Mignol would have gone to Dunlop, Goodyear, or Firestone. He would have concluded, with good cause, that Michelin was doomed, since we were hostile to innovation.

IVAN LEVAÏ: Does the company promote the idea of being better than the competition?

FRANÇOIS MICHELIN: The so-called market economy, or rather, the economy of responsible choice, as I would put it, has the enormous advantage of putting the boss's pride in its place. Our products are not always the best, nor are they always the cheapest. And when a customer chooses Goodyear over Michelin, it brings you down to earth in a hurry.

IVAN LEVAÏ: Is being "Number One" important for the company?

FRANÇOIS MICHELIN: The most important thing is to be the *best* whenever possible. But being "Number One," "Number Two," or "Number Three"—is it really that important? And besides, it really depends on the economic evolution of the countries where our main operations are located! But it is true that performance is measured by comparison with others. We latched onto a fabulous opportunity. Our competitors did not believe in the radial tire. Goodyear and Firestone did, in fact, buy the Michelin license, but they did not do anything with it. This should serve to make us modest about our success. It also shows the importance of innovation. At the time, the idea that we were leaving the industrial age to enter into a postindustrial era was already making its inroads, and many people no longer believed that technology has a future. This was an incredible ideological mistake made by old fogies in their mid-twenties who preferred to extrapolate curves rather than to put their faith in the human imagination.

YVES MESSAROVITCH: What thought process prompted you to make a decision that went against the trends of the time? You found yourself alone against a number of your management staff, alone against all your competitors. This being the case, you must have gone through some darned serious self-questioning when you were right and everyone was against you. Didn't you eventually ask yourself if you might not be wrong?

FRANÇOIS MICHELIN: It was not that I was right and that everyone was against me. I was right, on behalf of the customer. The customer needed a radial tire—and that was that. Nothing else counted.

YVES MESSAROVITCH: But perhaps there are times when you cannot be that sure of being right, on behalf of the customer.

FRANÇOIS MICHELIN: If the product is truly good for the customer and it can be put on the market at a low price, the case is closed. I am still astonished by the mistake that was made by our competitors. If Goodyear or Firestone had followed our lead, they would have become huge. It appears that it was financial experts who dissuaded them from developing the technology of the radial tire on account of its cost.

IVAN LEVAÏ: So mistakes do exist in industry, and you can end up paying for them a long time.

FRANÇOIS MICHELIN: That is the whole problem with the tire industry in Europe. It is obvious. As plain as the Eiffel Tower in the middle of the Champ de Mars.[13]

IVAN LEVAÏ: Have your competitors made up for lost time since their failure to capitalize on the concept of the radial tire?

FRANÇOIS MICHELIN: Absolutely. Many of them have once again become formidable competitors. We are now in a more normal situation in the industry. The owner of Bridgestone came from Japan at the end of the 1950s to see what was happening in terms of tire technology in France. When he discovered Michelin's metallic tire, he said to himself, *This is what I should be doing.* Now he is one of our main competitors. He is most fortunate, too, because in Japan, when you have an idea in your mind, it quickly takes concrete shape.

YVES MESSAROVITCH: You mean to say that over there everything possible is done to foster success in business?

FRANÇOIS MICHELIN: Absolutely. And this attitude of theirs is still a force to be reckoned with. It is this that will allow Japan to recover.

By way of contrast, gauging from the attitude of certain of our politicians, those of us who are manufacturers get the impression that we are the enemy. Is it that we are "politically incorrect"? The serious problem in this country is that, as soon as you venture to point out the realities of the situation, you are suspected of being political.

IVAN LEVAÏ: Fifty years after the war, the French industrialist still does not have the recognition that he should have. There is this atmosphere of extreme distrust, as if the bitter memories of the past (such as child labor, for example) were not quite forgotten. How do you explain this?

FRANÇOIS MICHELIN: People's perceptions of questions such as child labor or, more generally, social conditions at the beginning of the century—or even before—are often distorted. Read La Bruyère's descriptions of the hordes of peasants who were leaving their fields in the seventeenth century.[14] These people had only one concern: to forget the abominable conditions they were living in. The industry was a way out for them. Let us have the humility to acknowledge that we cannot judge matters that we have not lived through. This is not to say, though, that the solutions that were adopted were always the best ones.

IVAN LEVAÏ: But social victories have always arisen amidst pain and strife.

FRANÇOIS MICHELIN: I will not say that company executives, who are as human as anybody else, did not sometimes make mistakes. Even so, if you look at the year 1936, for example, it was, to all appearances, quite prosperous. But the inflation was horrendous!

One day my grandfather said to me, "I should have come up with the idea of paid holidays earlier." But, at the time, the economic circumstances made it difficult to shut down plants for three weeks. The sales were quite small. If you look at the films that were shot on the Champs-Elysèes in the 1930s, there are *no* cars! Unavoidably, in the past, the number of tires produced was much lower than it is today.

IVAN LEVAÏ: What relationship do you see between politics and business? If you look at the problem historically, you get the impression that very often it is politics that applies either the brakes or the accelerator to the economy.

FRANÇOIS MICHELIN: This is a complex problem but, basically, for me, the best kind of politics consists of giving each person the means to become what he is and to satisfy needs that are still unknown to him. This is a tendency that exists in the United States, in Silicon Valley, for example. Once again, it is the customers who are the subjects of the economy, and not the opposite. If you want politics to help in creating a healthy economy, it is necessary for citizens to become the subjects of the State, whereas, in point of fact, they are looked on as objects. People are viewed as "fiscal reserves," and the State is busy using them up.

YVES MESSAROVITCH: Do you find nowadays in France that people do not give enough thought to whole great areas of enterprise, which remain unknown? You mentioned Silicon Valley. Why is it that we do not have anything like it in France? Is it because of political or administrative roadblocks? Is it because we have essentially become Malthusians?

FRANÇOIS MICHELIN: That is possible. I have asked myself why, for example, France put so much time and effort into developing the telephone. In actual fact, it was Jean Monnet and his planners who decided that, because the telephone was a sign of social advancement, it had to be "granted" to the user.[15] "Granted"—notice the word that I am using and what it means! To fully understand things, you always have to go back to words and their meaning. One day, I went to see Pierre Mauroy, who was then prime minister, to speak to him about equity capital for business. As he had been delayed, I had a moment to spend in discussion with his secretary, Mrs. Boutillon. This discussion quickly got quite straight to the point:

"Ah, you are a man of money, of profit."

"Yes, that is true. But what do you mean by 'profit'?" I asked her.

"'Profit' is what you put in your pocket."

"Forgive me for being pedantic, but the etymological roots of the word *profit* come from the Latin *pro facere*. In other words, it is what you put aside 'in order to do or make something.' The peasant who does not put anything aside to prepare for his next harvest cannot get his job done. Actually, I am a man of money and profit because I am always thinking about ways to plan for the future."

"Well, in that case, I think we can agree!" she concluded with a smile.

A few minutes later, I spoke with the prime minister on the importance of equity capital for a business: "A business without equity capital can be compared to a runner who tackles a mountain while hooked up to an IV! Similarly, a soldier who goes to war thinking that he should come back with all the ammunition that he took with him will not last very long. It is the same principle in business. Without glucose in its system, a business cannot grow. And without ammunition, it cannot fight."

Is not the flexibility that equity capital gives also an outstanding way to avoid social instability?

Notes and Explanations

1. Limoges: Middle-size town in the center of France, famous for its porcelain manufacturing.
2. Antoine Gros (1771–1835): French painter.
3. William Bouguereau (1825–1905): French painter.
4. Strasbourg: Town in the east part of France near the German border, location of the European Parliament assembly.
5. Frederic Taylor (1856–1915): Wrote *The Principles of Scientific Management*, which studied the breaking down of tasks into their smaller components and the suppression of useless operations.
6. Twingo: Small, modern, and very inexpensive, recent model from Renault.
7. Xavier de Maistre (1763–1852): French writer and essayist, author of *Trip Around My Bedroom*.
8. Seine: River that crosses Paris from southeast to northwest.
9. Charles de Montesquieu: French philosopher and author of *Persian Letters and the Spirit of Laws*.
10. *Pneumatic*: Greek word meaning breath, air.
11. Malthusian—Robert Malthus (1766–1834): Anglican pastor who argued that human procreation must be slowed down to adapt to the earth's capacity to provide its sustenance.
12. Jura: Mountain range, in the eastern part of France, two hundred miles from Clermont-Ferrand, toward Switzerland.
13. Champ de Mars: Large area in the center of Paris, where the Eiffel Tower stands.
14. Jean de La Bruyère (1645–1696): French thinker and author of, among others, *The Characters*.

15. Jean Monnet (1888–1979): French economist, convinced General de Gaulle to set up central planning in 1945, which then led to the creation of the first European organizations.

2

Capitalism and Responsibility

YVES MESSAROVITCH: How would you define *capitalism*?

FRANÇOIS MICHELIN: Capitalism rests on an evaluation of the consequences that actions have. One way or another, every action carries sanctions that go with it. It is experience that has taught me this. And I realize that it is one's own experience in life that gives us the opportunity to enter into a real dialogue. That is why we are touching on realities here that do not necessarily have any political coloring to them, even a centrist coloring.

We are engaged in doing this book together, because we suppose—in all modesty—that we have a useful experience to communicate to people. The resulting work will be judged by the reader. Its sanctions will come in the form of its success or its failure. The same principle is involved when we turn to the market. A business comes up with a product and makes an effort to find out whether this product has any bearing on the real needs of the customer. In effect, the ruling question becomes "Does the shoe fit the customer's foot?"—not "Can we fit the customer's foot to the shoe?" If the answer to this question is "Yes," the product enjoys good sales, and the business receives money in return. The instrument that measures customer satisfaction is money. The market is the place where the consequences of a capitalist action are borne out—whether they be positive or negative. Someone who is in charge of a business is also accountable to his shareholders. He risks their money, but he cannot do whatever he wants with it. The purpose of management is to be forever verifying whether the investments made are profitable and whether, therefore, they are such that they ensure the future of the company on the one hand and a fair compensation for the risk taken by shareholders on the other. In a way, this process allows an assessment to be made of the foreseeable consequences that investments have.

IVAN LEVAÏ: It is true that every action has its consequences. But do you really think that the person who performs the action systematically desires its consequences to be verified and assessed?

FRANÇOIS MICHELIN: Human beings, I repeat, are the only self-teachable beings on the planet. In their hands they have all the means to better themselves, or to destroy themselves. To grow, they have to constantly weigh the consequences of their actions. Capitalism gives them this opportunity to be responsible.

The economic liberalism to which I subscribe gives people the conditions of freedom that enable them to gather experience in such circumstances that they cannot escape the resulting sanctions, in the fullest sense of this term. It is the only system that leads to a betterment of the common good. "The common good is the set of means that are necessary to satisfy needs that are still unknown," says Friedrich von Hayek quite rightly.[1] He adds: "At the heart of the market economy every human being is in search of his happiness. This is the invisible hand."

This vision of things is obviously diametrically opposed to the one espoused by the followers of philosophical liberalism, who reject any point of reference that is exterior to man. Once, a professor of history and geography said to me: "Mr. Michelin, the terrible thing about capitalism is that it is a natural phenomenon, not a creation of the spirit." Note the logic of the phrase he uses: "The terrible thing is that it is a natural phenomenon!" The rejection of any point of reference that is extrinsic to our own will, the rejection of any kind of judgment, a closing in on oneself and one's own system of thought, a rejection of all transcendence, this is the very essence of philosophical liberalism: "No God nor master nor reality." So, you can do anything whatsoever without being subject to sanctions. And it degenerates rapidly with the usual results: dictatorship. Dictatorship consists of rejecting the rules of life in society in order to impose one's own rules. It is a totally destructive system. In point of fact, however, the capacity for innovation and creation cannot find expression other than by reference to an objective "North Star."

The worst lie that a person can inflict upon himself is to refuse to ask himself questions.

Basically, philosophical liberalism creates individuals who are closed in on themselves and contribute nothing to the community. Economic liberalism creates the conditions whereby individuals become persons who enter into relationships with other persons.

Whether you see the other person as an individual or as a person changes things radically.

YVES MESSAROVITCH: Capitalism is built on trust.

FRANÇOIS MICHELIN: Precisely. This induces people to weigh the consequences of their actions well before they act.

IVAN LEVAÏ: But all the same, isn't there a basic conflict of interest between
the employer and the wage earner? The less I give my cleaning lady, the more I
get to keep in my own wallet.

FRANÇOIS MICHELIN: If you pay your cleaning lady poorly, she will not
stay with you very long, and you will have a lot of trouble finding a good one
afterward! There is no conflict of interest between the employer and the wage
earner, but, at the very most, there is a difference of interest that lies in the "here
and now" or in the long term. But the Marxists, who do all their reasoning in
their own little, closed universe, are incapable of integrating the notion of the
long term into their way of conceiving things. The capitalists, on the other hand,
quickly realized that if they wanted people to work properly, it made more sense
to foster their sense of responsibility and to make them partners rather than
"slaves" as rapidly as possible. Henry Ford understood this perfectly when he
decided to give his workers a substantial raise in pay—without penalizing his
customers by making his prices too high—in order to allow a number of them to
acquire a car. This is how American prosperity was born.

IVAN LEVAÏ: So, for you, capitalism is an ideal, harmonious world where
the interests of the "captains" contribute to the general well-being almost naturally?

FRANÇOIS MICHELIN: More than anything else it is a system that counts on
people and their capacity for progress. Once I read the following in a Leftist
weekly: "The vote on the law on abortion constitutes a victory over capitalism."
There you have it in a nutshell! The vote on a law that legalizes the separation of
an act from its consequences is a victory over capitalism! So, by implication, the
person who conceived this phrase meant to say that capitalism is a system that
links an action and its consequences. To dissociate one from the other is to reject
the whole point of education. Capitalism, in the non-Marxist sense of the word,
is basically a system that educates. There is another important aspect to be considered. Contrary to what this law on abortion might imply, what comes first for
these people is not the person and his personal greatness, but society. Now in the
ethical foundations of capitalism, the person comes before society. For me the
matter has no ambiguity about it at all: *Society is made for man, and not the
opposite.*

Of course, there are abuses, and mistakes can be made. But things like this
are penalized, inasmuch as the capitalist always has to face up to his responsibilities in a way that is practically irreversible. If he misses a turn, his car is
wrecked. As Simone de Beauvoir and Jean-Paul Sartre once said: "For the Left,
sanctions are collective, while for the Right they are personal."[2]

Within the capitalist system, a "plant" is a team. Advice should always be sought before action is undertaken. The team is there to inform us, to put us on our guard, to make sure that the business will stay the course and keep its place in the market. Furthermore, there is a tremendous instrument behind every capitalist that allows him to arrive at a finely calibrated measurement of the quality of his work: the honesty of his balance sheet as verified by the auditors—but this is an instrument judging after the fact. Meanwhile, every action that is performed in the business remains a reflection of the freedom and responsibility of the person who performs it.

YVES MESSAROVITCH: Does this imply a humanist philosophy?

FRANÇOIS MICHELIN: Of course. To live together, people need to respect each other. Freedom presupposes ethics, a morality; that is to say, a set of instructions that allow a definition of the code of behavior that should be adopted toward other people and with regard to oneself. You should not do to others what you would not want done to yourself. For this, you have to begin by arriving at an understanding of who you are. What is man? John Paul II says that man is the only being in creation whom God wanted for himself. The human being is unique. This is a marvelous thing when you think of it. I have always been deeply shocked that lawmakers pass legislation on embryos without ever giving a precise definition of what an embryo is. How can such a fundamental consideration be brushed aside? If you do brush it aside, you fall prey to philosophical liberalism, which legitimizes the gravest of actions under the pretext that the law allows it. This means that we no longer live in a state of law.

IVAN LEVAÏ: In 1941 a woman was guillotined because she was carrying out illegal abortions. It is terrible to take away a person's life because . . .

FRANÇOIS MICHELIN: That was the law at the time. The context has changed. But the abolition of the death penalty has not done anything to change the seriousness of the problem.

IVAN LEVAÏ: So, then, are you really denouncing philosophical liberalism and the notion of noninterference?

FRANÇOIS MICHELIN: You cannot have a system of complete noninterference, as if a person could do whatever he wants. Liberalism should let things take their course but with standards of measure to back it up. The ideal system allows people a wide scope of activity, at the same time reminding them that there are sanctions.

YVES MESSAROVITCH: How do you explain the great crises that have been the outcome of noninterference arrangements? Is this because there was too much of it?

FRANÇOIS MICHELIN: No, it is just that the standards of measure were broken, that is all. That was the case in 1930. It is the case today in Southeast Asia. It is a crisis of philosophical liberalism.

IVAN LEVAÏ: In the strict sense of the term, noninterference has never really existed. There have always been laws, be they just or less just, that have attempted to impose constraints on people and organize them. There is no example of a society without laws and regulations.

FRANÇOIS MICHELIN: You are right. But do these laws always take into account the complex realities of life? This basic law remains: Every man must be accountable for his actions. And this is not something that anybody else can do for you.

IVAN LEVAÏ: How did you interpret the critical remarks that the Pope made in Cuba about liberalism?

FRANÇOIS MICHELIN: When the Pope expresses his reservations about liberalism, he is attacking philosophical liberalism and not liberalism as the economists understand it. The two are utterly different. Philosophical liberalism rejects any kind of constraint and goes about refuting all notions of transcendence. The philosophical liberal thinks that his navel is the center of the world. Instead of opening himself up to others, he closes in on himself like an oyster and considers himself God. Economic liberalism, on the other hand, is a system in which people agree to live together in freedom and submit themselves to a common set of rules, which results in an economy based on the idea of contract—a social contract, as it were.

IVAN LEVAÏ: Nevertheless, the Pope does not hesitate to denounce the increase in poverty and readily stresses the need to share. These preoccupations are very much of an economic nature! Sometimes I even find he has a "sharing" side, to use an expression that was used in the past with regard to Marxists.

FRANÇOIS MICHELIN: Communism wants to "grab things by force." In the case of the Pope, he tells us to "give." This is where the difference lies. It is so much more beautiful and meaningful to give and to see the other person just as he or she is: a man or a woman. But the question is: What should you give? Some fish, or the *knowledge* of fishing?

Besides, the Catholic religion has nothing against wealth, as long as it is a means of enriching others as well. Saint Thomas Aquinas is quite definite on this point: "Riches that lie idle are like stagnant water at the bottom of a cistern."[3] *Everyone should put his or her talents at the service of others*, whether these talents be intellectual, emotional, artistic, or monetary.

As soon as the Pope defines man in his fullness and recalls man's end as a spiritual being, which is all too often forgotten, he is suspected of wanting to be a political activist. There is nothing political about giving a direction to life and saying that man has to be respected in order for him to remain rooted in truth. Respecting the traffic signs is simply making sure that you can make your turns safely.

YVES MESSAROVITCH: According to the dictionary, the person who is liberal is "favorable to civic and political freedom and to the general interests of society." The opponents of liberalism claim precisely the opposite.

FRANÇOIS MICHELIN: They are confusing true liberalism with philosophical liberalism. The latter actually verges on anarchy. Life is impossible without ethics and moral rules. The whole problem with life in society revolves around the establishment of true rules that are accepted by everybody and that point out the direction we should be moving toward. There are so many principles, which mark out boundaries, that ought not to be breached. That is why I am quite happy that the auditors have a control after the fact over the regularity and good order of the information we give out on Michelin's activities. In the same way, I consider it fortunate that Michelin's customers, by their free and responsible act of purchasing, have told us what they think of our products.

IVAN LEVAÏ: Speculation is an integral part of economic liberalism. Do you not think that to speculate is to show a lack of respect for human activity? Look at the Koreans and the Indonesians. There they are, ruined suddenly by the action of speculators.

FRANÇOIS MICHELIN: First of all, speculation is what happens when a person looks around him in an effort to anticipate events. You know, a meteorologist is a speculator.

Like any other word, the word *speculation* has evolved a great deal and become tainted with a pejorative connotation. It is a little bit like talking about wine while your eyes are focused on the mottled face of a drunk! We need to return to the primary meaning of words.

But to tackle this problem of speculation, I would need to make a longer and more elaborate response.

IVAN LEVAÏ: I accept the notion of speculation in industry—that betting on the future, which takes place when owners bring a new product onto the market, for example—but betting with money in order to make money can appear immoral. Sometimes the markets really overstep the bounds of reason. You see people there who do not believe in anything except money. Their only goal is speculation. They are the ones doing the harm!

FRANÇOIS MICHELIN: You are hitting on a fundamental point. This is an extremely complex problem.

If speculation, as you define it, closes the financial world in on itself, you are right.

But if financial speculation really gets its lifeblood from a study of the economic context, in that case it becomes useful and necessary.

"Finance" comes from the old French word *fine*, which means: to bring something to its end point, to finish. Hence, finance is a means.

YVES MESSAROVITCH: All the same, there are sanctions. A bank that makes bad decisions can collapse.

FRANÇOIS MICHELIN: That is true. It is an awesome business. If industry and the banks work together, risk can be minimized to ensure lasting growth. Once again, liberalism has absolutely no connotations of independence but is built, rather, on the establishment of free and responsible relationships. A person's hands are not independent from the rest of his body.

IVAN LEVAÏ: For more than fifty years, we have lived with an outlook characterized by class struggle. Despite this atmosphere of dialectical division, to a certain extent we managed to regulate our problems amicably. The exploiter was meeting with the exploited, and they had dealings with one another.

FRANÇOIS MICHELIN: The idea of class struggle was an unreal, virtual world. There are economic realities that you cannot avoid: The true owner of the company is the customer, not the owner. Does a person become an exploiter because he is buying tires?

The crowning idea of Marxism is the concept of the plan. Planning refuses to acknowledge the fact that the customer transcends the industry just as the taxpayer transcends the State.

IVAN LEVAÏ: Do you distrust the State?

FRANÇOIS MICHELIN: I distrust that particular form of the "sovereign" State, which cannot allow the possibility of experimentation. It decides everything. The business leaders are far from being perfect, but at least the capitalist system allows their self-sufficiency to be quashed and their errors to be mended. They are constantly subject to the judgment of financiers, their shareholders, and their workforce. If a worker does not like his boss, he should be able to go work somewhere else. This liberal way of doing things—which is to say "liberal" in the true sense of the term—is coherent. The day you put on the tinted glasses of Marxism and you suppose that there is a strongly dialectical and systematic relationship between men, you are getting into an absurdly destructive logic! Respect for others disappears. The problems take on a whole different light when you realize that there is a basic coherence in this world, in terms of which, every man needs others to live and develop. It is quite destructive, for example, to reduce political debate to the twin concepts of majority and opposition.

Aren't you journalists somewhat to blame for this as well?

YVES MESSAROVITCH: The two approaches are cut from the same cloth. Aren't they both sides of the same coin: a destructive side and a constructive side?

FRANÇOIS MICHELIN: Yes, but if you forget the constructive aspect of things, you will never get anywhere.

IVAN LEVAÏ: Here you are touching on the limits of liberalism.

FRANÇOIS MICHELIN: Liberalism consists of looking upon the other as a unique being and not as a subordinate. There is a story that I am fond of recounting and that still moves me deeply. One day at my office in Clermont arrived a man who was about to retire. He told me that he had come to that same office, when he was sixteen, to deliver a letter to my grandfather who was then seventy-eight. "Come on in, sir," my grandfather said to him, "and please take a seat." In the years that followed, the man never had occasion to return there. "His calling me 'Sir' has stayed with me all my life," he explained to me. And we conversed about the meaning of the word *Sir*. Etymologically "Sir" is a shortened form of *Sire*. To address someone as "Sire" is to acknowledge that he has within him something uniquely irreplaceable and transcendent. If we do not look on every individual as *Sire*, we are missing something essential. This is true for everybody from top to bottom, from worker to owner, from union leader to politician, without any exceptions. As soon as you no longer look at someone as having this potential, this marvelous seed that he carries within him, you are killing yourself without even knowing it.

YVES MESSAROVITCH: If it comes from somebody who is sincere, addressing a worker as *Sir* is an impressive gesture. Conversely, have not many businesses used this as a smokescreen to mask certain unpleasant realities? Such an approach has sometimes caused what is pejoratively called "paternalism in the workplace." Perhaps in these instances it is because the worker did not have enough counteracting power to fight against it, don't you think?

FRANÇOIS MICHELIN: To speak of a "counteracting power" is meaningless. Can there be power without real responsibility? To my way of thinking, that is dictatorship. Is there such a thing as counterresponsibilities in business?

IVAN LEVAÏ: You do not deny the usefulness of engaging in some sort of social dialogue in business. And you accept the idea of a social partnership.

FRANÇOIS MICHELIN: I do not know what the word *partner* means when it is paired with the word *social*. Are the owners part of this social aspect? The present climate that surrounds this issue tends to foster the belief that the union and the workforce are one and the same. It must be noted that in the course of real life this is not the case. Besides, you only have to look at the growth of coordinated groups of workers who reject the exclusive protection of the unions.

What is a good union? What is its responsibility? Let us look at the dictionary: "Partner: someone who has the same end in view as you do." Is this the case?

A "social" dialogue should be conducted directly with the personnel. It is a direct exchange between persons; everyone should come out of it enhanced in one way or another. Why? Because each person has his own specific traits and talents. Like statistics, a collective entity is a lie.

I have always had the impression that a union lives and acts as if it were outside the business and apart from it. It was Mr. Kaspar, former secretary of the CFDT,[4] who, at a *L'Expansion* forum,[5] illustrated this problem for me when he used the following phrase: "Now that we have acknowledged the legitimacy of the employers, it is high time that they acknowledged ours!" It must never be forgotten that unions are supported by the State. What is the nature of the relationship, by way of the State, between politicians and unions? What would happen to this relationship if social legislation was not framed to their liking? In your opinion, what significance does the unions' declining audience have? Why do trade union officials need to be protected if they are truly providing a service to the community? And what do you say about the auditing firms that are attached to the unions?

A union member once said to me: "Mr. François, you have to listen to what the unions and union members are saying; they will give you a temperature reading: They are a thermometer. But, you know, a sick man has never been cured with a thermometer." We shook hands and, lost in thought, I left him, saying to myself: *What could we do to free up enough time to establish a real network of contacts between the different actors in the company?*

I am struck by the dedication of certain union members. I have known and still know some outstanding ones.

IVAN LEVAÏ: A good union co-manages the business, which is to say that it takes into account larger, group interests. If there is growth happening and if productivity is improving, wages increase the same as dividends, and the union says "yes" to things. And the good union also says "yes" when a need arises for workers to put their nose to the grindstone and accept a pay reduction.

FRANÇOIS MICHELIN: "Co-management," to co-manage—what does this term mean precisely? To manage is to take on human, financial, and legal responsibility. No union does that. Note, too, that in talking about the role of the unions you have not mentioned the customer.

The exercise of power without responsibility is dictatorship. The exercise of power with its attendant responsibilities then becomes service.

Marxist unions reject the human reality of the market. Now while the union is elected only by workers, the business, for its part, is elected every day by its customers. The "economic" democracy is based on elections too! It is the whole workforce that is elected each time someone buys a tire. And this vote that the customer casts gives him a certain commitment, since he has given a part of his own substance to the product.

IVAN LEVAÏ: Do you remember that scene in *Zola* where, during a mining strike, the workers come to their employer's office and are terribly intimidated?[6] The parquet floors are polished. Cap in hand, they shift their feet awkwardly. It is a humiliating scene. Can paternalism really be genuine and sincere?

FRANÇOIS MICHELIN: You are forgetting something. How can a person not be impressed by the tasks that others assume? I am always intimidated when I go into a workshop.

Paternalism consists of the notion that, since people have nothing—and you have everything—you have to give them everything. It is thinking that you know better than they do what is good for them. This is what paternalism is.

What a difficult subject, however! Was the institution of family allowances—and Michelin was among the first to do this—paternalism? What about Michelin schools?

The best approach lies in teaching people how to fish rather than to give them fish and in explaining economic realities, to allow each person to come to an understanding of things and make his or her own judgments. This way, people can do something with what they have been given.

As for paternalism, the technocrats set a good example of it in their turn. "I think," they say, "therefore you are." Recently we received a letter from a government ministry (I have kept it) who said it is high time to organize relations between the elite and business! What does being one of the elite mean? Surely it means doing your work well and blooming where you are planted. My reproach against bureaucracy, urged on as it is by the politicians, is that it has refused to concede business the means to be partners with the whole world. It prefers to bury us under all sorts of expenses and taxes!

IVAN LEVAÏ: In the life of a business, there come times when you have to let go some of your workers. Almost overnight, as it were, they stop being partners. This can be justified, in order to save the main body of the company, but even so, the moral problem remains unresolved. In a way, when you dismiss someone, you consign him or her to a void. When your name is François Michelin, how do you live with that?

FRANÇOIS MICHELIN: With difficulty, with great difficulty, that is for sure. Letting a person go is a fearful thing to do and all the more regrettable in that quite often such actions are made necessary by regulatory burdens or political decisions that have nothing to do with the business. When you lay off someone, it is because you really cannot do anything else. What is missing nowadays is a way to let people go in an atmosphere of dignity. You ought to be able to say to them: "Listen, two or three years from now, I will not be able to give you any more work. You are going to have to leave us. We are going to find ways to make this transition as smooth as possible. You can start looking for another job, and we will do all we can to help you find one." These days, this sort of approach is impossible in France, because you cannot make plans and look very far ahead. Whenever you are forced to let someone go, you are faced with a heap of unrealistic, administrative rules and regulations, especially if you are a company that employs more than five hundred people. If only they made fewer useless, unrealistic rules and regulations! Fortunately, you know, many government employees are beginning to realize this.

The real question that needs to be asked concerns each person's participation in the creation of wealth. When the government hires additional employees, then it raises taxes, which means that you have to lay off people in the private sector. Because the government employees are not used for tasks that are all that necessary, they do not always help create the conditions that are necessary for economic life. A business, on the other hand, creates true possibilities for shared wealth, and these possibilities, as we have already mentioned, are achieved once the product is sold.

IVAN LEVAÏ: There had to be rules and regulations put in place for the employers who were not behaving properly.

FRANÇOIS MICHELIN: Of course, here you get back to the notion of a minimally necessary framework, but many of the current rules and regulations are, in fact, opposed to the dignity of men and women.

Employers who think only of laying off people are not employers. Dismissing someone is a terrible human drama. When someone leaves the company, it is a part of our very substance that is going away. Believe me: Over the last fifteen years, and just about everywhere in the world, we have had to let a large number of people go. Each time we did it, it was a real ordeal for the company.

YVES MESSAROVITCH: Michelin has undergone a significant transformation in the last ten years, as have many businesses that have been forced by a competitive environment to undergo an evolution in order to survive. These days, does your company still give the nation everything it can in terms of wealth, prosperity, and social equilibrium? Or, on the contrary, has the status of the company been perverted as globalization forges it into a stateless structure that is no longer mindful of the sense of social vocation that was its guiding principle for a full half century?

FRANÇOIS MICHELIN: What a ten years it has been! Many profound and fundamental changes have taken place and they are not necessarily all that readily apparent.

We could have done much better if the legal environment that was forced on businesses had taken the reality of the situation into account. In France, capitalists have always been looked on as hardly better than leeches, people who had to be put in their place. I have never heard a clear expression of the fact that there would be no work without capital, nor growth in capital without work. It is all too easily forgotten that, if there is work out there, it is because people have taken risks. Not anyone can be a capitalist. You have to be able to accept everything even if it means the loss of your capital and your own earnings.

That is why, too, it is very important to keep a balance between institutional shareholders and the shareholders who are actually physical persons.

IVAN LEVAÏ: What is the most just—not to say, the least scandalous—way to reward the partners in an economic undertaking?

FRANÇOIS MICHELIN: A just reward is one that allows both the business and the people involved to grow. The buying power of the personnel is a key component in the economic well-being of a country. As for the issue of remuneration for the shareholders, which has often been poorly understood in France, remuneration is essential in creating and sustaining the entrepreneurial dynamism without which neither jobs nor wealth can be created.

Experience shows that, allowing for both good and bad years, the rate of economic growth is in the order of 3 percent over the long term. Every increase in wages that goes beyond a gain in productivity that is not linked to growth in volume is harmful. High-tech businesses are going under, precisely because they failed to consider what the future held for them in terms of real growth.

YVES MESSAROVITCH: Does capitalism do a good job of incorporating the notion of time?

FRANÇOIS MICHELIN: Of course. Indeed, this is one of its essential characteristics. The experience that is needed for people to grow takes time. The life of a business is basically an ongoing creation. To achieve a better response to the constantly changing needs of its buyers, it can only move forward by engaging in innovation in both the long and short term. Hence the importance of research, which requires time and, therefore, the importance of long-term support on the part of the shareholders, in order to finance these efforts and take repeated risks to ensure the growth of their capital. Thus, the three main actors in a business—personnel, shareholders, and customers—are engaged in an adventure together over the long haul. To approach the business from a merely financial point of view is a major danger.

The ecologists say that nobody has the right to do whatever he wants, as people's actions have repercussions on future generations. There is no one more ecological than a true capitalist. He spends his time weighing the future consequences of his decisions.

IVAN LEVAÏ: All the same, our rivers are polluted, our cars are not all equipped with catalytic converters, the debate about the diesel engine is still unresolved.

FRANÇOIS MICHELIN: Perhaps, but look at the progress we have made as well over the last forty years! Man is in a state of continuous experimentation. If you put a stop to all experiments simply because mistakes have been made in the past, you end up putting a stop to everything. Man is not in control of anything. The only thing that we really know is that we know nothing. The day that you think you know it all, you are dead. Man is always growing and developing, but he can only grow to the extent that he agrees to accept his responsibilities. It is an act of humility. Keeping one's two feet planted solidly on the ground. Doesn't the word *humility* come from the word *humus*, which means "soil" or "earth" in Latin?

YVES MESSAROVITCH: In ten years, France's GDP has risen around two thousand billion francs, which is an increase of about 35 percent. This is a significant increase, but do you get the impression that people's happiness has grown by a third in ten years? What has this growth given to individuals? How has it been socially "used"? The prime minister of Bhutan said: "You Westerners do your reasoning in terms of Gross National Product, but I reason in terms of Gross National Happiness." Has not the forward march of production created more discontentment than it has satisfaction? How else do you explain the quest for immaterial things on the part of many of our contemporaries?

FRANÇOIS MICHELIN: This dissatisfaction is a way or approach as much as it is a question. The Catholic Church offers a vision that says that there is no quantifiable, materialistic answer to man's irrepressible desire to be happy. This is extraordinarily profound. The Catholic faith makes people humble. Are there other religions or other systems of thought that can lead us so well to the threshold of the mystery that we are—and make us feel that this mystery has a real meaning, that it is not opium?

IVAN LEVAÏ: It is you industrialists who have made our happiness a material one. Nowadays, when I take my car, I am not too hot nor too cold; I listen to the radio, I drive on a paved highway, I sit in a plush, comfortable seat with a nice carpet under my feet, and within arm's reach I have a guide that tells me which are the best restaurants to stop at along the way! Mr. Michelin, in a way, it is you who have pushed us toward a life of ease.

FRANÇOIS MICHELIN: The industrial, scientific world has put you in the position where you realize that comfort, good tires, and a nice car are not enough to nurture your soul. There you have it! The ultimate goal of economic and scientific development is to show man that there is something that transcends him. Bluntly put, you have come to realize that you have everything and that you are nothing because you are lacking what is essential. "Let the splendor of the world teach you that you have been created for much more than this," I remember reading somewhere. In short, Saint Augustine says: "Our hearts are made for You, O Lord. Until they rest in You, we shall be restless."[7]

IVAN LEVAÏ: Does this justify your passion for technology?

FRANÇOIS MICHELIN: Do you mean to say that the thing that is essential is to be seeking boundaries that are always receding indefinitely?

The Bible says that it is the mission of craftsmen to complete creation. Isn't this marvelous? The only real way to approach God is through beauty. *Beauty is the most beautiful prayer.* This is true in all areas. There are some impressive passages in the Bible: "They have seen Creation but have not returned to the Creator." Or this psalm: "They think that I do not see them, whereas it was I who made their eyes."

YVES MESSAROVITCH: In your mind, then, are beauty and perfection one and the same thing?

FRANÇOIS MICHELIN: Exactly. "A good airplane is beautiful," said Marcel Dassault.[8] A beautiful plane or a beautiful car can kindle a kind of transcendence, as long, of course, as you do not make them idols or ends in themselves. An object will never give you full satisfaction. Oftentimes, before you acquire something, you dream about it, you tell yourself that it will be great to have it. And then, when you get it, you are well-aware that the happiness you were expecting is not complete. There is something missing. Man is a "capacitor" made to be filled. The more you learn, the more hungry and thirsty you are for something else. It is inexplicable, but that is the way it is. Anyway, God cannot be comprehended by the intellect. On the other hand, the intellect can discover signposts that lead to God and the proofs for his existence. All of this is beyond understanding. When you want to explain God, you are not really explaining anything at all; the day that you think you understand what God is, you have really understood nothing. God, the self-subsisting being, says of himself: *I am the good that diffuses itself. I am who I am.* It is the episode of the burning bush. The intellect slips and slides as it grapples with the words of God, yet it never stops seeking until it reaches the point where it realizes that all it can do is fall on its knees and say: *It is!* It is the same as believing you have got someone figured out, believing that you understand him completely, and then discovering one day that you do not really know him: Everyone is infinitely more than his visible, palpable, earthly exterior.

YVES MESSAROVITCH: You attach a lot of importance to the beauty of creation. For you, a worker is first and foremost a "craftsman," isn't he?

FRANÇOIS MICHELIN: Precisely. Even those who fulfill the smallest of tasks are accomplishing a work of craft. Following the death of a factory worker, who had passed away after having been treated by a bad surgeon, my grandfather created a hospital in Clermont. The company was taking great care of the cleanliness of the institution. To respond to this concern, the architect had the brilliant idea of devising the rooms in such a way so as not to create right angles between the walls and the floor but, rather, to round the bottom off. There were no corners, which made the task of the janitors a great deal easier. To give them a better understanding of just how important their job was, some dust was collected from a sick man's room and cultured on a petri dish. It illustrated how quickly the microbes contained in the dust could grow. After that, the housecleaning duties took on an utterly new significance. For now you were dealing with janitors with a capital *J*, who were accomplishing a work of craft every day.

IVAN LEVAÏ: As beautiful as an object may be, it should not make us forget God; and in order to *have*, man should not forget that he also needs to *be*. That is all well and good, but following on the collapse of ideologies, you get the impression that the utterly material world in which we live leads people to have more and more all the time and to forget about their need merely to *be*. Basically, is not man's alienation quite as great as it ever was?

FRANÇOIS MICHELIN: For man to experience his being, he has to *have*. That is the whole meaning of work. Also, you can always be seeking to have more, and thus you forget being and reject the mystery of your own self.

Being and *having*. To be able to couple these two words, it means that you have to have your own being, doesn't it?

But this dualism between being and having is a phony debate. When you *have*, you also experience that you are lacking something. Something of a different order. And that is when you are prompted to just simply *be*.

YVES MESSAROVITCH: This is what makes the world go around, doesn't it? You always want more.

FRANÇOIS MICHELIN: I would not put it that way. Man is made for infinity. How do you think he could be satisfied with finite "products"? To aspire for more is in the order of being. The path that leads to the achievement of this end is part of the mystery of every man and every woman.

IVAN LEVAÏ: All the same, you are not forgetting that it is earthly food that has made the *Michelin Guide*'s fortune and is still doing so.

FRANÇOIS MICHELIN: And that it is earthly food that gives pleasure to your nose and taste buds? Certainly I am not forgetting!

The *Michelin Red Guide*'s fortunes rest on the keenness of the French taste.

YVES MESSAROVITCH: Without revealing all the secrets of the *Michelin Red Guide*, the way that it can make or break an enterprise, could you tell us how you succeeded in generating the implicit trust that people have in it, such that it is generally recognized as a code of good conduct?

FRANÇOIS MICHELIN: One of the strengths of the *Michelin Red Guide* is that its readers know that we are on the lookout for things that are not as they should be. Oftentimes they write to us to give us their opinion or to rectify a judgment made by one of our inspectors. The success of the *Guide* is due to the fact that we are forever dissatisfied. Every year we receive up to a hundred thousand letters from users who mention their criticisms. Like art critics, we express our judgment, but we surely do not believe that we are the absolutely final reference.

YVES MESSAROVITCH: That is what gives rise to the trust that people have in the *Guide*. You sniff out deception and deceit.

FRANÇOIS MICHELIN: It is the love of progress and improvement that makes it necessary to sniff out problems and mistakes. In this regard, the anonymity of the *Guide*'s inspectors is essential. I, myself, do not know their identity, even though I might be acquainted with some of them from Clermont who may have wanted to change careers and, hence, joined the ranks of our inspectors.

Notes and Explanations

1. Friedrich von Hayek (1899–1992): Austrian economist.
2. Simone de Beauvoir (1908–1986) and Jean-Paul Sartre (1905–1980): Marxists writers and philosophers, advocates of existentialist theories.
3. Saint Thomas Aquinas (1225–1274): Philosopher and theologian.
4. CFDT and Jean Kaspar: Confédération Française Démocratique du Travail (French union); Jean Kaspar, president of the union between 1989 and 1992.
5. *L'Expansion*: Well-known French economic weekly.
6. Emile Zola (1840–1902): French writer, author of, among others, *Germinal*, mostly known for his position on the Dreyfus affair and for his request for a retrial.
7. Saint Augustine (354–430): Theologian and philosopher.
8. Marcel Dassault (1892–1986): Owner and president of Dassault Industries, the French aeronautical company that made the Mirage and Rafale jet fighters and the Falcon range of aircraft.

3

France and Globalization

YVES MESSAROVITCH: Is it your impression that the opening up of national borders, which was both desired in some respects and imposed by force of circumstances as well, is being carried out too rapidly in comparison to the adaptive capacity of a country like France? In your opinion, can the French afford to go head-to-head with world competition?

FRANÇOIS MICHELIN: Business is willing to compete but, unfortunately, not the government! It is sad to say, but in our country, there is a marked preference for hitting people with all kinds of duties and taxes rather than giving them the means to invent, to make progress, and to compete. This is the hub of the problem. French industrialists, I am convinced, are totally open to globalization. For some time now, the French economy has been oriented toward foreign markets, partly because we have to, since we do not have many of the raw materials that we need (oil, iron ore), but these days our technocrats are overcome with a feeling of panic in the face of globalization. They are discovering at long last, with humiliation, that our economy is dependent on the outside. For years they have denied the role that industry plays. Now that they are beginning to believe in it, they are discovering that France is just a small company in a very active world. It has been a rude awakening for them. It is true that they have never really seriously studied the question, except to put forward the false idea that France should have specialized in products that were costly and technically elaborate and left the manufacture of goods with a low added value to less-developed countries. Some of them even went so far as to say that our economy should be "spared" the industrial stage and, thus, go right from a primary to a tertiary economy. Fortunately, they realized in time that there are no jobs without industry. But our technocrats are still managing France like a young man with money who never asks himself how his family actually created its wealth.

The confiscatory tax laws applied to capital got worse in the 1960s, with the last straw being the tax on capital. This served to weaken the human fabric of French capitalism considerably. Behind the official noises—and I would like to know why, strangely enough, this has not unleashed a tide of media stories—the reality is that more and more French businesses are being bought by foreign investors, and this is not the fault of the shareholders any more than it is of the owners! It is the fault of the politicians.

In France, you have to pay the price to remain a shareholder. It is a shame, because the French have always shown that they can be innovative and are not afraid of hard work.

IVAN LEVAÏ: So you do not believe in a possible division of production, at least, if not of labor? Is there not an advantage, nevertheless, in having some countries specialize in certain manufacturing processes and forget others?

FRANÇOIS MICHELIN: To manufacture complicated objects, you have to have skilled people. Now, not all countries have the people with the necessary skills yet. Should they be banished from the world stage because of this? Also, let us not forget that in the so-called developed countries there will always be poorly skilled people. They, too, ought to be able to find work, even if it turns out to be traditional occupations or menial, little jobs, which are, I can add, quite as respectable as any other. I do not know anybody who is not happy doing good work. *It is every man's joy to succeed in something.*

So it would be a serious mistake to divide up production between the advanced and developing countries by a decision made at some sort of Yalta-style summit.

YVES MESSAROVITCH: What is bred in the bone comes out in the flesh: In the past, England nearly killed its industry, and now we have a situation where it has become more profitable to set up production there than in France. In the 1970s and right up to the first half of the 1980s, the Americans also had the notion of putting an end to their industrial capacity. Surely it is the height of irony that in our day they have become competitive once again. In France, industry is penalized by the heavy weight of costs and benefits—but can't we hope that one day the political class will bow to the reality of the situation and acknowledge that it has made a mistake?

FRANÇOIS MICHELIN: Even at the height of its Labour Party phase, England held on to the favorable infrastructure of transmission of patrimony, and to offshore companies that allowed individual and industrial patrimonies to thrive despite political options that were chosen as a result of obscurantist pressure on the part of unions and technocrats. The wealth that was thus protected played an essential role afterward in financing the reconstruction of the country—a reconstruction that was briskly carried out by Margaret Thatcher. One of the causes for the success of the English recovery is the basic rejection of union dictatorship. Our financial executives are now flocking to London. A hundred thousand French people have already settled there.

In the United States, things are a bit different. One fine day, a certain Mr. Sloan, who was CEO of General Motors in the 1960s, even went so far as to announce that the world had entered a postindustrial era. And thus, the students at Harvard were taught that in the future all that one would have to do is put some chrome on cars and do some marketing in order to sell them. And then the day came when the Americans were forced to embark on their cultural revolution, to face up to the competition from Japanese car manufacturers. But this revolution was only made possible because of the fabulous amounts of money that had been amassed in capital pension funds. Today, these are the funds that finance the American economy, to a large extent. In France, unfortunately, we do not have such pension funds at our disposal. Given these conditions, how do you embark on a recovery process similar to that of England or the United States? Without money, we no longer exist. All the young people who are leaving to try their luck abroad understand this quite well. They keep quiet, but nonetheless they vote with their feet.

YVES MESSAROVITCH: If you had to make a bet on the chances of our country's bouncing back, would you be optimistic?

FRANÇOIS MICHELIN: France has everything it needs to pull through, but I do not know how long it will take. Everything will depend on the humility of our political leaders. Will they be honest enough to acknowledge that they were mistaken in their analysis of the causes of our difficulties? Will they be clear-sighted enough to make a judgment about the situation in our country vis-à-vis international realities?

In any case, the hurdles to be overcome are enormous. By propounding certain ideas, we have allowed in our country a concept of economic life that is extremely restrictive, one that is based on the desire to bring employers to heel. . . . In fact, the spirit of class struggle prevails on every level of our social life, and the sheer weight of intellectual dictatorship that we are subjected to is alarming.

YVES MESSAROVITCH: Do you think, as François Mitterand has said, that we have done everything we can against unemployment?

FRANÇOIS MICHELIN: Yes, in the sense that we have used every available remedy to treat the wound superficially, but nobody has ever tackled the primary cause of the infection. How can businesses do more hiring when the social charges that they are supporting have gone up by 22 percent over ten years?

During this same time, the State has continued to increase the taxes borne by households, simultaneously reducing their purchasing power. Instead of making the cake larger and increasing the amount of work available, they have made the choice, quite simply, to slow down growth. It is a little bit like wanting to launch a hot-air balloon after you have slipped a noose around it—a huge rope that stops the balloon from expanding! Whatever success France has enjoyed up to this point is owed to the exceptional dedication of its businessmen and business-women. It makes me mad when I hear politicians say to employers: "Stop asking for money; get down to business." They have taken everything away from us, and then they are surprised that we feel we are being suffocated to death. And, as if that were not enough, this year again we are being forced to pay that idiotic surcharge, the trade tax,[1] a real brake on hiring and investment. Business is taxed even before it has created any wealth. If you put a mill next to the spring and not along the river, its wheels will never turn! To recover, France needs once and for all to get rid of the Marxist concept of existence that is prevalent in our society and which still inspires a number of supposedly elite minds. For them, the State is the referee and the employer is the enemy. This is outrageous! The Mattéoli Report laid it out quite clearly:[2] The basic cause of unemployment is the heavy hand of the State in our economy, but few people want to look this truth straight in the face. "The city mouse recites his lessons while the country mouse looks around and sees things," as Michel Serres puts it quite nicely.[3] France is a seed that only needs a little bit of water and sun to grow, but these days the money well is dry and the protective shadow of the State is obscuring the light of the sun. If, starting at the top, people were firmly resolved to stop throwing a monkey wrench into the works, the French would manage all of Europe! The potential that the French people have is extraordinary. Give them a free rein!

IVAN LEVAÏ: Don't you get the impression, though, that common sense is in the process of gaining the upper hand? Even the Socialist François Hollande has said that the thirty-five-hour week should not raise false hopes.

FRANÇOIS MICHELIN: Too late, the evil's been done! People have it in their heads that the thirty-five-hour week is going to lessen unemployment. When they realize that it is an insane, illusory hope, they will turn against the politicians and call them liars! The notion of a thirty-five-hour workweek is a perfect example of an ideological approach.

IVAN LEVAÏ: The sentiments you are voicing are not just confined to the employers. There is a feeling of protest in the air in this country. The people feel that they are being forced to yield to an all-powerful government which imposes all kinds of heavy-handed pressures on them.

FRANÇOIS MICHELIN: Let us not forget that the French, to use an accepted expression, are "subjected" to the Social Security System. This term, *subjected*, reveals much about the state of mind of the politicians who came up with it.

They have transformed what was supposed to be social solidarity into a kind of slavery. If you consider the primary meaning of the Republic's motto: "Liberty, Equality, and Fraternity," it leads to an impasse. For people to be brothers, they need a father! Equality does not have any meaning, either, if you confuse it with egalitarianism. When the notions of Liberty, Equality, and Fraternity are viewed as something that comes from outside of man, in the end they are transformed into either a dictatorship of the proletariat or an extraordinarily powerful technocracy. The French people are treated as objects of solidarity and not as subjects of solidarity. This attests, in actual fact, to a contempt for the people. This distinction between subject and object is essential, and your interior attitude as either a subject or an object often influences your success or failure. Notice what happens when you are confronted with sickness! What is your attitude? Is your focus on being sick, or on the sickness? Which matters more: the sick person or the sickness? We all know that the will and desire to get better may have a significant impact on the sickness. Subject or object?

YVES MESSAROVITCH: Because we are involved in the globalization of trade, will not France, sooner or later, have to adjust? Isn't a certain form of economic organization going to be imposed, whether we like it or not?

FRANÇOIS MICHELIN: Clearly. Until the present day, we had always been able to maintain a certain independence with respect to the outside world. Today we have lost this. What will I do if one day I receive a letter from a foreign pension fund and a Michelin shareholder asks me not to make any more investments in France because charges and taxes have become too high and the thirty-five-hour workweek is intolerable? We are trying to compete economically. It is strange that nobody really wants to acknowledge this.

IVAN LEVAÏ: Are we definitely going in this suicidal direction?

FRANÇOIS MICHELIN: We are not going there. We are already there. Over 40 percent of the shares in our finest businesses, those of the CAC 40,[4] are already held by foreign investors. Do not forget, too, that there is a movement under way to impose typically Anglo-Saxon notions of corporate governance on French businesses. These have nothing to do with age-old French law and the structure of French businesses. Do we want to kill off the very soul of France completely?

IVAN LEVAÏ: What can countries do when they are faced with this situation? Multinationals are all-powerful and dictate their own terms. In the dispute between Boeing and Airbus, America and the European governments have almost no say in the matter.

FRANÇOIS MICHELIN: If I do not want to buy *La Tribune* or *Le Figaro*, the State cannot do anything to force me. If somebody does not want to buy our tires, I cannot do anything to make them buy our tires, either. It can never be stressed enough that *the customer is the real owner of the business.* He is the one who decides to buy your products . . . or those of your competitors because yours are too expensive or not as good. If you forget this, the "thermodynamics" of the exchange is doomed to failure, unless you do some authoritarian planning and put your opponents in the Gulag or in concentration camps.

YVES MESSAROVITCH: But the power of the large groups is such that more and more often countries have to submit to their demands.

FRANÇOIS MICHELIN: A group's power comes from the quality of its trade and of its products. Why should not it be the same in the case of countries? Our leaders should convene the employers and ask each of them what should be done to make it possible for them to take up the battle on equal terms with their competitors in their respective sectors of the economy.

IVAN LEVAÏ: They are going to ask for subsidies!

FRANÇOIS MICHELIN: No, it is something entirely different that is needed for France's economic life. Ask yourself the question: Where does the money for subsidies come from? From taxes!

A government that distributes subsidies to everybody is not worthy of the name. I am not opposed to the principle of subsidies, but there should be some justification for them, and they should be distributed in such a way as to make people aware of their responsibilities in return.

YVES MESSAROVITCH: Which brings us back to the idea that subsidies are a good way for the State to establish its power.

FRANÇOIS MICHELIN: The problem of power is knowing what to do with it. For what end is the power being used? What are the responsibilities associated with it?

IVAN LEVAÏ: You can understand why the State gives subsidies to agriculture. We very much need to preserve "France's garden." But what about other sectors of the economy? In ten years more than a hundred billion francs of aid has been given to the steel industry, for example. Hasn't this gone too far?

FRANÇOIS MICHELIN: The tragedy of the iron and steel industry stems from the European Coal and Steel Community. Instead of asking employers what they needed in order to go to battle, the government made the decision on its own to keep certain businesses alive artificially—with, obviously, the rigidity and inflexibility that naturally goes with it! What good did it serve if, at the end of the day, all they have managed to do is manufacture a product that cannot be sold because it is too expensive?

IVAN LEVAÏ: Do you think that our country does enough to encourage innovation?

FRANÇOIS MICHELIN: That is a good question. The answer is somewhat sad. Innovation is not encouraged at the level where it should be. The real reason for this, I believe, is that France does not have the mental and financial structures that are necessary for innovation. Until quite recently, it was almost impossible to obtain venture capital in France. How do you expect the national banks, which do not have their own capital funds, to be able to take risks with their depositors' money? It is unthinkable. Hats off to all the industrialists and their shareholders who have managed, in such difficult conditions, to do what they have done in France! It is extraordinary. If they had had a mere tenth of the financial resources available to the Americans, Europe would be French!

YVES MESSAROVITCH: François Mitterand chose to open, wide, France's borders within the framework of GATT and then the World Trade Organization, but internally we have not taken the overall measures that would allow us to fight on an equal footing with foreign competitors. How do you account for this shortsightedness? And what consequences do you see arising from it in the future?

FRANÇOIS MICHELIN: Mr. Mitterand was right to open up the borders. He was hoping that this would wake up the politicians, but this is happening much too slowly. Right now our situation is as follows: It is below zero-degree Fahrenheit outside, the doors are wide open, and we are being asked to take off our sweaters! Michelin exports 50 percent of its products outside of France. This is twice the national average. Thus, half the total wages is tied to operations that are outside of France with the result being that everything that penalizes us with respect to our foreign competitors, in terms of quality or price, has fatal consequences for at least 50 percent of the company's manpower. The thirty-five-hour workweek, for example, is leading us straight to a disaster. I have nothing against working fewer hours, *but not if this raises the cost of our tires.* All of France's budgets should be analyzed on the basis of this criterion.

IVAN LEVAÏ: One gets the impression that the adjustment is being made by sheer force. On the one hand, the State is in decline and growing weaker. On the other, globalization is advancing by leaps and bounds with no end in sight. . . . And all the walls and barriers are collapsing. Today, if I want to make a phone call without going through France Telecom, I can.

FRANÇOIS MICHELIN: This whole process can only increase the freedom of individuals and businesses. And French politicians have a very hard time accepting this. It is true that the power of the State declines when it is not fulfilling its task!

YVES MESSAROVITCH: Why?

FRANÇOIS MICHELIN: I have no idea. You have to want other people's freedom, you have to desire to give them the capacity to conduct experiments and to make mistakes sometimes as well. The State does not like this idea very much. One of the biggest difficulties of an employer is allowing the people facing a problem to freely express themselves so that they can choose the best and most realistic ideas. From this point of view, the State has some progress to make.

IVAN LEVAÏ: Are not French businesses also responsible for this state of affairs? Here, as soon as something is not going right, people turn to the State. The immediate reaction of the Americans, on the other hand, is to try to sort things out on their own without appealing to the authorities.

FRANÇOIS MICHELIN: The fault does not lie with industry. It lies primarily with the State alone and its will of power. The moment that you no longer want to give others the means by which they can be themselves and make progress, because of the market, and the moment that you want to establish your power at any cost, you wreck the whole system. Of course, men make mistakes. They are far from perfect, and sometimes they make errors, but their sense of responsibility enters into play, and corrective measures are quickly put in place. The vast number of small errors made by all the actors in the economy as a whole is infinitely less dangerous than the major mistakes committed by a dozen technocrats working in their own little areas of responsibility. Look at the drastic mistakes made by the planners in Moscow or by the circle of people around Hitler! What do you expect? Our governments do not like alternative ways of looking at things. This is their great flaw. As soon as you bear witness to facts, which show that the theory in place is no good, you are accused of playing politics. It is said that the Pope is being political because he maintains that, according to Christianity, man is what structures society, not the opposite. What is the Gulag other than a rejection of an alternative way of thought? And, unfortunately, it is clear that third-party judgments and decisions have much more weight than judgments and decisions made by those who are in close contact with the reality of any given situation.

YVES MESSAROVITCH: Where do you draw the boundary line between the desire to gather and unite and the risk of domination?

FRANÇOIS MICHELIN: This is a problem of ethics, of love in the strongest sense of the word. You become a dictator as soon as you no longer acknowledge the fact that the other person has a part of the truth.

YVES MESSAROVITCH: In a way, the fight against inflation can be considered a kind of economic dictatorship. Nevertheless, it does have its virtues.

FRANÇOIS MICHELIN: Inflation is the granddaddy of all vices. Keynes, who obtained the financing for Hitler's national socialism from the Bank of England, said it quite well: "I am an immoralist because I know that inflation is able to pervert the conscience."[5] Inflation is an organized lie. A drug that can have tragic consequences. Wages rise, investors can no longer make investments, nobody wants to lend money.... In this respect, one of the basic virtues of Mr. Trichet's politics is that it forces us to make a real, true effort.[6] A strict money supply forces us to confront economic demands and, thus, put up a fight that goes in the right direction. In this case, it is not the law of the strongest that is imposed but the law that stems from the reality of things. If, in tomorrow's world, we no longer have an industrial efficiency that is on par with that of the Americans, we will no longer be able to export.

YVES MESSAROVITCH: What about the taxpayer? Doesn't he also play a prime role?

FRANÇOIS MICHELIN: Certainly. Only here is the rub: The American taxpayer has much more power written into his Constitution than does the French taxpayer.

In France, when people talk about lowering taxes, they say that it is going to cost the government! Where is the taxpayer? What happens to his purchasing power, the foremost element in economic life?

IVAN LEVAÏ: Globalization favors acquisitions and mergers and transnational organizations. How do you avoid being bought out one day by those who are the richest and most powerful?

FRANÇOIS MICHELIN: You cannot do anything. The tragedy is that successive governments, beginning with Joseph Caillaux,[7] have all made it impossible in France to accumulate money. Their fear was that people might have too much independence vis-à-vis the State. Antoine Pinay, who was an intelligent man, gave business the means not to have to go abroad, thanks to the fund that bears his name.

IVAN LEVAÏ: How do you view your competitors? Are companies like Pirelli and Goodyear potential prey for you? Or are they rivals to spur you on?

FRANÇOIS MICHELIN: Like us, they are actors in an extremely competitive market in which the customer is always looking for improvements. It is simply a matter of offering prices that are lower than theirs for a better-quality product.

IVAN LEVAÏ: All the same, any victory on your part would mean their defeat.

FRANÇOIS MICHELIN: Would it be a victory? Anyway, there are times when you are tempted to crush all the competition, but it often cannot and should not be done because, behind every business, there are people. And also, as you know quite well, a customer who has only one supplier stops using his brains. The absence of competition leads to a phenomenal loss of substance.

YVES MESSAROVITCH: Are not we all to blame for allowing monopolistic conditions to have developed?

FRANÇOIS MICHELIN: I do not believe so. As soon as you take too much money from customers through excessive taxes, these customers get poorer and start to want to buy cheaper products. To achieve the lowest price, therefore, manufacturers are forced to adapt and get into mass production in a big way. So you become "too big" against your will.

YVES MESSAROVITCH: In that case, why don't taxpayers and consumers have a more responsible attitude and do more to protest this situation?

FRANÇOIS MICHELIN: Whom should they protest against? Their minds have been polluted.

YVES MESSAROVITCH: It looks likely that the advent of open borders is going to trivialize everything: production processes, social relations, and finance and taxation systems. Don't we run the risk of losing something of our cultural identity in all this?

FRANÇOIS MICHELIN: No. When you build a road that everyone can use, this does nothing to weaken the individuality of those who drive on it. A change that affects everyone does not mean homogenization. There is no doubt that globalization is going to prompt us to revise the way we think and change some of our habits, but it is also going to give us a new relationship with reality. This new connection is going to give the French a strength and a dignity that are much superior to the sort of cocoon that they live in today. Why should you call it "trivialization"? On the contrary, this is a salutary, cleansing process!

YVES MESSAROVITCH: The United States, that is at the height of its economic, financial, and military might, has never had fewer doubts about its position in the world today. Nor do the Americans really have much desire to do any kind of cleansing. American political correctness, moreover, betrays the total absence of any kind of meaningful debate on the other side of the Atlantic. Is not this reluctance to engage in any sort of self-questioning also a form of trivialization?

FRANÇOIS MICHELIN: I do not agree with you at all. There is an extraordinary debate over ideas in the United States. It is France that has not done enough in terms of self-questioning since 1947. It is very difficult to begin questioning yourself and to admit that you took the wrong road. There is a great, big cow in the room. The only ones who cannot see it are our ideologists.

IVAN LEVAÏ: They see the cow but do not dare grab a stick to chase it out. Despite all this, though, do not you have the sense that we have made some progress? People are not blithely opening up all kinds of doors and windows anymore with impunity. . . .

FRANÇOIS MICHELIN: Alas, we are still in a dense gray fog of ideas. Nevertheless, the North Star is there to suggest the way that we should follow.

This does not mean that we should rush ahead without giving things a thought. We can move forward, swerving sometimes to the right, sometimes to the left.

YVES MESSAROVITCH: Is the creation of the Euro likely to accelerate the adjustments that have been imposed by globalization?

FRANÇOIS MICHELIN: Don't you see that the technocrats are preparing to put in place a shell that will not by any stretch of the imagination be enough to change things! The Euro is not a solution in itself. Whether or not there is a single currency, the real question posed by globalization remains in fact the following: "What do we need to do, so that France can compete and so that our businesses can perform well and go off to conquer new markets?" We know that the real engine of growth would be a massive lowering of public spending, which means lower taxes. This is the only way to give customers back their purchasing power and to make it possible and desirable for them to buy, save, and take risks.

How long will the French people be able to afford the luxury of a town council, a general council, a regional council, a House of Representatives, a Senate, Strasbourg, and Brussels? Governments should provide an example in saving money—but that is not what they are doing.

IVAN LEVAÏ: The Euro is supposed to serve as a sort of safety railing.

FRANÇOIS MICHELIN: You cannot decree the value of a currency. When a country's economic activities are not as good as those of a neighboring country, its money depreciates in value. The Euro will do no good if the governments involved do not start taking some measures that are absolutely vital, moving forward together toward a more flexible approach, less spending, and fewer taxes.

YVES MESSAROVITCH: In the economic and monetary union that is coming, good systems of taxation should force out the bad ones. Don't you think that the French will win out in this respect?

FRANÇOIS MICHELIN: What is necessary, first and foremost, is an intelligent management of public spending. Then we need a system of taxation that is intelligent as well, one that allows for growth.

Notes and Explanations

1. Trade tax: Tax set up in 1975, based on the rent value of the total assets and on the total manpower cost.
2. Mattéoli Report: Jean Mattéoli (1923), French politician, member of the Social and Economic Council.
3. Michel Serres (1930–): French philosopher.
4. CAC 40: French equivalent of the Dow Jones; takes into account the shares of the forty biggest French companies; Michelin belongs to the CAC 40.
5. John Maynard Keynes (1883–1946): British economist.

6. Jean Claude Trichet (1942–): French economist and head of the Bank of France.
7. Joseph Caillaux (1863–1944): French president of the Council of Ministers, as was called the post of prime minister under the Fourth Republic.

4

Not Enough Economic Thinking

YVES MESSAROVITCH: A recent study put out by the OECD has shown that, although experiments with a shorter workweek have sometimes created jobs, they have not, by and large, generated additional wealth. By setting up the thirty-five-hour week in France, do we not risk seeing the country sink into a state of self-complacency?

FRANÇOIS MICHELIN: France has not yet coped with the additional fifth week of holidays and the thirty-nine-hour workweek, launched in 1968. Wealth can only be created when you are selling. For me, the implementation of the thirty-five-hour week will have a negative effect on consumption. To go from a thirty-nine-hour workweek to a thirty-five-hour one, with no reduction in wages, would amount in effect to an 11 percent increase in the payroll, which will indirectly increase the cost of the products—in the end, resulting in a decrease in the purchasing power of the people. Then they will reduce their purchases, and the creation of wealth will suffer because of it. The effect of this will be to slow down growth. After totally jamming up the works, you will have no choice but to get it going again. How? Through inflation! But the central banks will not tolerate this for very long. They will raise interest rates.

IVAN LEVAÏ: The thirty-five-hour week does not have to be construed as a demand for more comfort and leisure, as was the case with paid holidays, for example. These days, people want to share their work with those who do not have any. Somehow it is a legitimate, noble demand, almost Christian in its inspiration.

47

FRANÇOIS MICHELIN: True sharing happens when every person actively makes use of all his gifts. Life in society—particularly, life as it is lived in the world of industry—is not a zero-sum game. The true form of sharing that should be promoted sees every person being enriched, so to speak, by the sharing he contributes to. There has to be growth on the economic level and on the human level. If you do not make this your basic objective, that is to say, if you start from the principle that it is a zero-sum game, the result that you will be left with will not be solidarity but poverty and social strife. So, it is by aiming to give every-one the means to work more that you will facilitate the sharing that people aspire to.

YVES MESSAROVITCH: In this debate about the thirty-five-hour week, are not people rightly seeking to develop their talents? If they want more free time, is not it in order to have the time to do what they really want to do in life?

FRANÇOIS MICHELIN: That is true. But they must not lose sight of the fact that, without money, these activities are unthinkable. And the less you work, the less money you make. It is only logical. There is something in this debate that utterly appalls me: Everyone is in agreement about having machines do more of the work, but people forget that *what people have in their heads is infinitely superior to all the machines in the world.* For materialists, the mind does not exist as a spiritual entity. It is simply a manifestation of matter. France has become a materialistic country. It is more concerned with dividing up the pie than with creating it.

IVAN LEVAÏ: How many hours do you work every week?

FRANÇOIS MICHELIN: And what about you? What is work? Once this ques-tion was put to a little girl. She answered: "To work is to build." What does it mean, "to build"? It is to give yourself a target that you want to reach. It is find-ing materials to build a house or to produce tires. You think that you are building a family or a company. And, in the final analysis, it is yourself that you are build-ing. In my own personal case, I believe that I am working all the time. To work for a business is to always keep its objectives in mind, to assimilate anything that can help you clarify them, and to find the means to achieve them.... It is also to ask yourself why things are the way they are. When you have properly under-stood the reason why things are what they are, you know how to make use of them. Reasoning by analogy is a marvelous tool. Quite often, different phenom-ena have something in common that connects them—an underlying, primary cause that allows you to understand a lot of things. You may merely be watching someone sweep the street and you can suddenly be struck by an idea that will allow you to improve the machines that you use to make tires.

IVAN LEVAÏ: Do you think that the State should be in the business of legis-lating on the subject of working hours?

FRANÇOIS MICHELIN: Abuses need to be avoided. That is the role of the State. But the problem of the thirty-five-hour week is different. Let us have the courage to admit that laws like this touch on the freedom to work and on the freedom and responsibility to do business. I might add, too, that this law, which has already been passed but which will only achieve full implementation in several stages, is contrary to democracy. They want to divide and distribute a pie that the thirty-five-hour week is going to make smaller. How do you expect employers to accept a decrease in purchasing power by putting a cap on wages? With all this, there is no possibility of growth. As always in France, the egalitarian vision takes precedence over any other consideration.

One day I had a discussion about the SMIC[1]—a monstrously heretical thing to do—with a government minister on the right wing of politics:

"You give the impression that the government can increase the purchasing power of the people in an arbitrary way, that everything depends on the goodwill of the government," I told him. "You are no longer linking remuneration with effort. But whether you like it or not, it is a basic given of human activity."

He replied that he would prefer someone to be unemployed rather than to be working for less than the SMIC. Nevertheless, if a man is not active, if you are paying him to do nothing, you are destroying him. This is the whole tragedy of unemployment—and people accept it, all for the sake of an insane ideology of egalitarianism. Without the SMIC, companies—notably, small and medium-sized businesses and industries—could do much more massive hiring. All you would have to do is leave them in peace. Nor is there any doubt that, in the end, many wages would exceed the SMIC.

IVAN LEVAÏ: What does "leaving them in peace" mean for you?

FRANÇOIS MICHELIN: First and foremost, you would have to give them sane, realistic laws. In France, the employment laws have drawn their inspiration from Marxism. They were developed by Ambroise Croizat,[2] a member of the Communist Party. For the most part, they rest on the underlying idea of class struggle. They are Soviet-style laws. According to their logic, business is a closed system from which the customer is curiously absent. In reality, of course. the customer is at the basis of everything. By contrast, in a closed system, the owners and workers are cast as masters and slaves, and they oppose one another on a philosophical level. This being the case, the State imposes itself on the scene as the compulsory referee, with sweeping regulations whose primary effect is to cut the bonds that link human beings. These bonds are essential to the existence of business. Thus, they destroy the very thing that makes for the magnificent, manifold beauty of humanity: free, unhindered relationships between people.

YVES MESSAROVITCH: This closed system was put in place with the complicity of the employers, the government, and the unions. Is not everyone guilty?

FRANÇOIS MICHELIN: That is one of the reasons why Michelin left the CNPF at the time of the Grenelle Accords in 1968. In 1966, I was not able, in spite of all my efforts, to put the word *consumer* in one single, solitary declaration of the CNPF. The other reason is that, before François Perigot,[3] none of the officials at the CNPF cared about the "shareholder." Does not the employer exercise his responsibility in relation to three groups of individuals: the shareholders, the customers, and the workforce?

IVAN LEVAÏ: When you quit the Employers Association, did you do so on your own or with other employers?

FRANÇOIS MICHELIN: Businesses are not registered directly in the CNPF. It is the Association of the Rubber Industry that represents us with the CNPF's authorities. We simply told the rubber industry association: "Either you withdraw from the CNPF, or we are leaving the association." At the time, all the other employers muttered to each other: "What is the matter with that fool from Clermont-Ferrand?" When you live in Paris, you do not have enough critical distance to have a clear perception of the reality of things. Life in Paris, with its orientation toward the "Country Club Economy," tends to impose uniform thinking, simply because it is often cut off from the rhythms of flesh-and-blood reality.

IVAN LEVAÏ: Is an association for the employers really very useful?

FRANÇOIS MICHELIN: I find it quite revealing when people say that the head of the CNPF is the "boss of bosses"!
To have an organization, independent of politics, to explain the reality of the world of business is indispensable, but for all too long this has not been the case.
But do not forget: We, at Michelin, have the same boss as our competitors, Goodyear or Pirelli. The customer! When a car manufacturer tells us that he wants a tire for a car weighing 1.5 tons, which is going to go 120 miles an hour and has to be able to transport four people, he is giving us an order in the true sense of the word. If we do not provide him the tire that he needs, he will go someplace else. This is where the basic principle of the "economy of choice" is to be found. It is the best system there is in terms of confronting people with their responsibilities.

IVAN LEVAÏ: The fatigue that workers suffer has also changed in nature. It is not a matter of aching muscles anymore. These days, people suffer from nervous fatigue.

FRANÇOIS MICHELIN: In Clermont we use very sophisticated machines. After four or five years, some of the people who work on them ask for a change of scenery. They cannot stand the fact that all they are using is their brain, which is only one part of their existential makeup as people. They are no longer satisfied with the job of being an overseer. This is indeed a difficult problem!
That is why all the talk to the effect that French industry should concentrate on elaborate, sophisticated products, and leave to underdeveloped countries the

task of manufacturing simpler, low-grade products, does not hold water. What do you do with individuals who are not able to work on complex machines? They are just as much worthy of respect as the others, but they are going to be cut out of the picture. It is the responsibility of the State to reflect on the way in which the production costs of business can be reduced, in order to allow people to continue working in the textile industry, for example. The solution is simple: You have to reduce charges and taxes. Everyone knows it. What is the Balladur or Juppé subsidy if not an acknowledgment that cars cost too much?[4] Free zones have been set up, but what does this mean, other than that outside of these zones the State's levies are too high? These indirect admissions of failure should be taken very seriously, and their significance needs to be pointed out. This would make a wonderful topic for the media.

YVES MESSAROVITCH: Everyone concedes that taxes on wages and capital are too high and that they will have to be lowered massively in order to reduce unemployment. The problem is that, in doing so, you risk causing the fragile house of cards to collapse. Out of fear, successive governments have been content to tinker with the old machine, even though it is in bad shape, rather than overhaul it from top to bottom. This being the case, how do you carry out the necessary reforms while at the same time respecting the European context of the situation without causing a cataclysmic, national upheaval? Do we have to wait for the whole thing to break down massively before the decision is made at long last that it needs to be fixed?

FRANÇOIS MICHELIN: The problem is that we no longer have a statesman who is capable of saying: "You have an illness. It has to be taken care of, if you do not want to get worse and end up with something more serious—a heart attack, for example." Fish always start rotting from the head down. People are getting bogged down in sterile debates between the Right and the Left. The real question is, getting a handle on what must be done so that within their limits people can grow and bloom where they are planted and be given the means to become what they really are. That is the real question. The answer can only come from questioning that monstrous phenomenon of State-imposed authoritarianism, created by the politicians, which France suffers from. France suffers from a planned economy. The politicians have given the bureaucrats free rein in their desire to run the whole show. The thinking in this country has been that the bureaucrats are more intelligent, more concerned about the public interest than are the citizens. We have not been able to make them realize that the public interest stems from the sum of all the particular interests. As if there could be a public interest that is not the sum of particular interests! Contempt for the role of the employer reached a peak with the price controls that President Renè Monory, who was then minister of Finance, started to impose at the end of the 1970s. This price control cost us phenomenal sums of money. Prices were frozen while, at the same time, there were rate increases in Social Security contributions, electricity, et cetera.

IVAN LEVAÏ: It is also a contempt for the market. It is a refusal to recognize that natural law of the market, the law of supply and demand.

FRANÇOIS MICHELIN: Yes, it is a contempt for buyers, the supposition being that they are not responsible and are incapable of making a good choice. There is a confusion on the part of some of the French people. For example, somebody in the company once requested his supervisor to ask the boss if he could intervene with the government with a view to changing the law of supply and demand. Nobody had pointed out to him that the law of supply and demand is a reflection of reality and, thus, a natural law. You are right. The refusal to recognize natural law and reality is at the root of our country's difficulties.

YVES MESSAROVITCH: Is not it also a way for the upper echelons of the government employees to protect their own interests and keep their prerogatives? We have lost our colonial empire, but we have kept control of the French economy.

FRANÇOIS MICHELIN: I would not want to read into their intentions. I think that these upper echelons really believed that the State had to intervene. In the 1960s I made a proposal to a member of the steering committee of the ENA,[5] suggesting that on-the-job training in the business world be organized for the students. This was his reply to me: "You are going to distort their judgment!"

Upper-level government employees have a very highly developed sense of the public interest. They are decent people. They have a sincere belief in the regulatory function of the State. They are not totally wrong, but what a shame it is that, in their training, they have not been given the chance to exercise any of the real responsibilities that responsible businessmen must exercise. They would find out that only the customer is in a position to know what he wants. The function of the State is to take this reality into account.

YVES MESSAROVITCH: We have been taught the very opposite. Take the State plan, for example, which really amounts to a desire to set up signposts in the future.

IVAN LEVAÏ: In itself, the State plan is a Soviet-inspired notion.

FRANÇOIS MICHELIN: Absolutely. The notion of State planning, which entails determining six years in advance what the citizens should be buying, is fundamentally antirepublican and Marxist in essence. Anybody who talks about freedom is really talking about freedom of choice. Of course, you have to have the means with which to achieve this freedom.

This is not to say that you should not make projections into the future, nor that any initiative by public authorities and economic players acting in concert should be rejected from the start. It can be said that there are two types of planning processes. The first, State planning, considers the citizen as an object. The other, which is essentially liberal, considers the person as a responsible subject, that is to say, the motor of a society that is driven by an infinite diversity of personal needs.

IVAN LEVAÏ: We are scared of the global economy. At every turn, we risk being devoured. We are the hens, and the fox is the American or Japanese economy. We are in a global economic club where it is very hard to lay down rules and where, in the name of freedom and free trade, the most powerful have the most leeway in their actions.

FRANÇOIS MICHELIN: Why couldn't we be powerful players as well? France is still thinking: *France only*. It is her great failing. Do you want an illustration of this? Take the question of the trade tax. In an economy protected against imports, the fact that we are the only country to have a trade tax appears on the surface to be of no consequences for the short term. In fact, this is not true, for as soon as it becomes possible for people to buy foreign goods, the trade tax becomes a subsidy for the imported goods. The problem is that nobody cares about this state of affairs. And so the trade tax remains in place, causing an increase in unemployment and a rise in the cost of investment. Local government as well as chambers of commerce are busy killing the hen that lays the golden eggs. The introduction of the trade tax was a political act, not an economic one.

IVAN LEVAÏ: Here you have something that the employers could mount a fight against. Why didn't they rise up more aggressively against this tax on employment?

FRANÇOIS MICHELIN: The CNPF was a political organization for a long time. Its chairman was regarded as a government minister for the employers! Hence, his being called "the boss of bosses." This is changing, which will be very good for France.

IVAN LEVAÏ: We have State-controlled agriculture and sectors of industry that are subsidized, and now we are subsidizing employment. Is not one of the reasons for France's misfortunes to be found in the fact that, in our country, everything is subsidized?

FRANÇOIS MICHELIN: I am afraid so. It is the result of a Marxist concept of society. From this point of view, Louis XIV and Colbert,[6] like Hitler and so many others, were "Marxists." There is something else, too. We had a remarkable man in the company who said to me one day: "I have made a great discovery. I was taught in school that the reason that the world is in such bad shape is that it is not run by people as smart as we are. But I have since discovered that there was another factor, one that did not fall into the domain of logic and reason: man's freedom when he is faced with the good or bad things that he can do. I realized that logic and reason did not work when faced by this factor. I had been steered toward a theoretical, virtual world. This was not the right way to go." Another person once said to me: "You remember Fourastié and his theories about the primary sector (agriculture), the secondary sector (industry), and the tertiary sector (services).[7] We had thought that France should avoid the drama of undergoing the industrial stage in its economy and go directly from the primary sector to the tertiary sector. And then, we made a big discovery: We realized that there were no jobs without industry!"

For me, this was an explanation as to why I was not succeeding in getting our message about industry across to the government. Quite often the people in government have a concept of economic life that does not correspond to reality.

YVES MESSAROVITCH: And why do young people in our schools, universities, and post-secondary institutions not learn enough about production? It is utterly absent from the curriculum, as if it were something that is degrading and shameful. Are there still lingering echoes of Zola in people's minds? Is this because of an intellectual snobbery?

FRANÇOIS MICHELIN: One of the leading Marxists once said to Lenin: "You are making a mistake in developing your educational and training programs. If you teach people how to reason, one day they will realize that they have been deceived." It must not be forgotten that our national education system still works under the Langevin Report.[8] Consider, too, our modern mathematical training, which tries to promote reasoning about concepts rather than realities. Now when you introduce people into the domain of concepts, you can manipulate them exactly the way you want. A concept allows you to demonstrate anything you want and its opposite, and that is, how you turn out slaves who arrogantly believe that they are masters. One day I went to see President Georges Pompidou to let him know that modern mathematics would be the downfall of France. "Do you know how Pascal discovered geometry?" I asked him. "By looking at the parquet lines on the floor. Had he been taught modern mathematics, he would never have discovered geometry. With this sort of education, we will not have decent chemical engineers or doctors anymore. We will have an approach to medicine that is conceptual and drug-oriented but not a practice of medicine based on observation." Fortunately, this is in the process of changing. The notion of clinical study is regaining its importance, but we are behind other countries. Certain aspects of American medicine are outstanding. In Clermont, there is a chiropractor who goes to the United States regularly for refresher courses. I suggested to someone who had a knee problem and whose doctor was threatening to send him for an operation that he should go see him. Ten days after he had gone to visit this chiropractor, his knee was completely healed. All the chiropractor had done was to press on a small area of one of his vertebrae and unjam the whole thing. He had been able to see immediately that, if the knee was swollen, it was because it was out-of-whack and not working properly. He had gone back to the cause of the ailment in order to treat his patient. There is no doubt that this modern world of ours always mistakes consequences for causes, especially in France. Thus, modern mathematics and set theory are the result of a long, scholarly process that is of some use to certain brainy types, but for the majority of people, it does not make any sense. What purpose does it serve to put someone on the top of a mountain that he does not know how to get down from? As soon as the Russians noted the failure of modern mathematics, they abandoned it—lock, stock, and barrel— as did the Americans as well. And, as luck would have it, or so it seems, this is where science is making the most progress. Current estimates show about forty thousand French engineers who have left France to work in Silicon Valley. It is not a case of mere chance. There they have the opportunity to achieve fulfillment and to grow in a climate of realism.

YVES MESSAROVITCH: In social matters, theory can sometimes be found to be opposed to reality, but you get the impression that the realism that tempers the minds of the employers needs to be better articulated. As it stands, they are at a loss for words that are needed to combat the inapplicable model that the politicians want to impose on them. To win over public opinion, don't you have to return to the truly basic questions such as the whys and wherefores of production, who you are producing for, and at what cost?

FRANÇOIS MICHELIN: Very much so. In the company there was a Communist employee whom I had known in the past. He was a former friend of mine from my army days. The two of us found ourselves together at a class reunion in Savoie,[9] and we entered into a very free-ranging discussion, as we had in the past.

"Your supervisors really p—— me off!" he said to me. "They are always asking me to work more, as if it did me any good!"

"How much do you think the company earns when it sells an off-the-road tire?" I asked him.

When I gave him a rough estimate of our profit margins, he confessed to me rather pensively: "I had absolutely no idea that the company is so fragile."

Another time, I was trying to explain what capitalism is to a worker who was asking me. I started by pointing out a number of things to him but realized at a certain point that he did not understand me because there was a key element missing in his reasoning process. I asked him if he had money in a savings account or a bank, and he said that he did. I wanted to know if he was paid interest on this money, and he said that he was, around 3 or 4 percent at the time. At that point, I asked him where, in his opinion, the money for the interest came from. His answer to this was clear and simple: the Bank of France. It was the Bank of France that made the money to cover the interest on the capital that he had in his account. When I explained to him that the money that was needed to pay his interest came from the fact that his initial capital had been lent out to businesses like ours, he exclaimed that "surely, [he] was costing the company some money!" He was caught up in a system of thought in which there was no relationship of cause and effect, an unrealistic system that was totally ideological and utterly socialistic. Then I wanted to know if he could play the lottery with borrowed money. He said, no, since, if he did not win, he would not know what to do to pay the money back. I put the following hypothesis before him: If an engineer came to you with an excellent idea that had a 50 percent chance of success, would you agree to develop this idea with borrowed money? Again he said, no. If the idea was not a success, he would not be able to pay back either the capital or the interest. I told him to imagine that he was the engineer in question and that someone told him that he was ready to advance him some money and then win it or lose it with him. He replied that, in that case, he would do it. So, there you have the essence of capitalism. Here the real role of the shareholder comes to light. It revolves around the necessity of allowing men to try things out and experiment. It is important to realize that this complementarity of roles constitutes the very foundations of an extraordinary progress and growth in economic life.

There is another story yet that I was very impressed by. A lady who worked as a secretary in one of our plants in Nova Scotia in Canada once explained to me why she had left her previous employer:

"The owner of the store where I was working fired me because I was expecting a child." She was convinced with all her heart that this man was a downright SOB. But what struck me was that at no point did she have anything to say against the capitalist system. In France, an employee faced with an identical situation would inevitably have said: "The capitalist system is rotten."

IVAN LEVAÏ: Do you think that here in France, at the end of the century, capitalism remains a disputed question?

FRANÇOIS MICHELIN: Yes, absolutely. One day I was listening to an outstandingly intelligent philosopher supporting the creation of a kind of "coordinating committee" whose role would be to avoid the "abuses" of competition and set up a sort of regime of corporatism.

At the end of his lecture, I simply asked him: "But what about creating some sort of coordinating committee for literature? When I go into a bookstore, I am always struck by the number of books there are crammed onto the shelves. There are just too many of them. Nobody has the time to read them. It would be the job of this coordinating committee to select those that are worth a go, and as for the others." He reacted sharply to this suggestion and cited freedom of expression and creativity.

In fact, all that an individual asks for in any society is to be given the chance to express what he has to say and to be given the freedom and the means to put it into practice. Intellectuals express themselves by writing books. As for us, we express ourselves by making tires. That is all there is to it.

IVAN LEVAÏ: Are you quite certain that class struggle is still going on? Many Frenchmen no longer dispute the fact that some people own the means of production and others are wage earners. Within the companies, social dialogue is actually occurring. Possibly, the only points of dispute concern the organization of the workplace and how the profits arising from growth are to be shared. Moreover, even though employers may be having second thoughts about certain features of what is considered social progress, or workers may be calling for a sixth week of paid holidays, the notion of class struggle, properly speaking, no longer enters into the equation.

FRANÇOIS MICHELIN: Our country suffers from a lack of practical, economic culture. Consequently, it is very difficult to have a calm, dispassionate dialogue. The arguments of the employers do not carry any weight. Many people still have loads of preconceived animosity toward them. Every time there is a discussion, you have to sit down at a table and explain the whys and the wherefores of things and the delicate balance that exists between the cost of products and purchasing power. You are forced to establish the connection that exists between what you give your shareholders and what you give your employees.

One day, at the gate of the plant, I had the opportunity to enter into a discussion with a union representative who was handing out pamphlets. I have forgotten his name, but I do remember that he has very blue eyes.

After an exchange of views that lasted at least twenty minutes, I asked him: "As far as you're concerned, is an employer a worker?" He replied immediately: "No, because an employer doesn't have worker's status!"

To define a man according to whether or not he has a certain status—what a strange way this is to look at life! He justified his answer to me by maintaining that a worker takes orders, something that is obviously not the case when it comes to an employer.

At that point I explained things to him: "When automobile manufacturers, for example, turn down our tires, aren't they, in effect, ordering me to make products that are less expensive and of a higher quality? When my quality control department rejects a certain raw material as inadequate, isn't this also the same as my being ordered to go out and buy a better quality product that is easier to work with?"

In the end, when all was said and done, it turned out that I am a worker!

I wonder if this conversation does not serve to highlight an essential aspect of the difficulties that our country is experiencing. It is this aspect that lies at the roots of our social breakdown. The definition I was given of a "worker" is eminently Marxist and would ordinarily lead to slavery. Fortunately, the reality in industry is utterly different.

We should simply note that many political attitudes stem from the presupposition that the employer lives on another planet and is not a worker.

Each and everyone has responsibilities of the same nature. We are all pursuing the same objectives but doing so in different ways and in different geographical areas. The notion of class struggle is a wonderful pretext for consolidating political power in a planned economy.

YVES MESSAROVITCH: Considering that the economy has been under a spotlight in the media over the last twenty years, you would think that certain messages might have become stale by now.

FRANÇOIS MICHELIN: It is very difficult to have any sort of exchange with ideologists, whether they be left-wing or right-wing. They take their point of departure from ready-made approaches, concepts that are far removed from reality. They have not reached the stage where they can admit that there are people who think differently from them. They are prisoners of a system of thought to which they ascribe the transcendence that is lacking in materialistic approaches. Just as AIDS patients have lost their immune defenses, people who are "suffering from" Marxist philosophy, for example, have lost any point of reference. It is so effective at closing individuals in on themselves that the other person, by definition, becomes an enemy. Reread the Satanic poems of Marx: You will understand how sick and corrupt this philosophy is.

IVAN LEVAÏ: You would have thought that the spectacular collapse of Communist society was going to put things back in perspective. Who could still call himself a Marxist, in the face of such a monumental disaster?

FRANÇOIS MICHELIN: Those who still believe in it claim that Communism is a deviation from Marxism. They absolutely refuse to call into question the materialistic analysis of life in society. Marxism remains an extraordinarily powerful form of messianism. And for what results!

IVAN LEVAÏ: Do you really think that Martine Aubry is a Marxist?[10]

FRANÇOIS MICHELIN: Who am I to judge? You know, we are all more or less Marxists at certain times in our lives in any case. The essence of Marxism is the rejection of the other. Marxism is a kind of intellectual virus that can strike anyone, sometimes without his knowing it, Christian democrats no less than radical Socialists, Communists, moderate Socialists, and members of the so-called Right. All of them draw their inspiration from the same source. For all of them, the State is better able to manage society than individuals themselves. Marxism rejects two of the most fundamental questions there are: "Where do we come from?" and "Where are we going?" Held hostage by a system of thought that is totally absurd, man has no choice other than to resort to the State in terms of transcendence. In that case, he risks becoming no more than a little bug caught under the crushing weight of a steamroller.

YVES MESSAROVITCH: What do you think of the training in economics given in the schools today?

FRANÇOIS MICHELIN: All you have to do is open the economics textbooks in our national educational curriculum to realize that Marxist ideology is far from dead. If anything, the situation has gotten even worse. Some political officials are busy reestablishing the conditions favorable to class struggle.

Also, what a huge number of engineers there are who, with five years of experience under their belt, are critical of their training for having cut them off from an important part of reality!

IVAN LEVAÏ: Should a worker at Michelin know the company's financial accounts? In an ideal business, should an X ray, so to speak, of the business's financial state be information that everyone has access to? Would not this be a response to the lack of economic training that people have?

FRANÇOIS MICHELIN: In 1930, the company was on the brink of bankruptcy. My grandfather had a certain Mr. Vigier go around to the banks to ask them to loan us money. He came back with what, in today's money, would be equivalent to a billion francs and went to see my grandfather in his office. "I have the money," he said with a delighted expression on his face.

"Good thing you do, Mr. Vigier," my grandfather replied. "Had you not gotten it, we would have been bankrupt." In retrospect, Mr. Vigier collapsed to the ground.

There are very few people who can hold up under the pressure of a high-risk venture. You cannot and you should not tell everyone everything. You have to take into account each individual person's ability to understand. The way that people receive information depends on who they are. On the other hand, too, there is always the risk that the information that is given to the employees may fall into the hands of the competition. This can be deadly to a business.

IVAN LEVAÏ: Aren't you the "last of the Mohicans"? You are at the same time a name, a family, and a flagship, and it may be that you are the last surviving French name brand for a world-renowned product.

FRANÇOIS MICHELIN: I hope not. You know, when you begin to get just a glimmer of understanding that each person is unique, I really do not see how you could view the problem in terms of being "last of the Mohicans."

Notes and Explanations

1. SMIC: Salaire Minimum Interprofessionnel de Croissance; minimum, State-controlled base salary, for all professions.
2. Ambroise Croizat (1901–1951): Communist minister of labor from November 1945 to May 1947.
3. François Perigot (1926–): President of the CNPF in 1986.
4. Edouard Balladur and Allain Juppé: Names of two French prime ministers who heavily subsidized the purchase of new cars in the 1990s.
5. ENA: Ecole Nationale d'Administration (National Administration Institute). Created in 1945 under de Gaulle to serve as a specialized institute to train upper-echelon government employees.
6. Jean Baptiste Colbert (1619–1683): Minister under Louis XIV, believer in a powerful State.
7. Jean Fourastié (1907–1990): French economist, author of *The Great Hope of the Twentieth Century*.

8. Langevin Report: Named for Paul Langevin (1872–1946) Marxist French physicist, advocate of the fact that studies should be mainly theoretical, cut from reality.
9. Savoie: Province of eastern France, close to Italy, two hundred miles from Clermont.
10. Martine Aubry (1950–): Several times minister of labor and social affairs until 2000.

5

The Boss—The Man

IVAN LEVAÏ: The Michelin adventure is fantastic. Your family has put its signature to a product, much like the artist who signs his canvas. After more than a century, your name is world-renowned to the point where it has almost become a generic term. There are many people whom such popularity would have made vain and conceited. How can you live through that with simplicity?

FRANÇOIS MICHELIN: I do not look at the distance we have already covered but, rather, at what we have yet to do. That helps to keep a person's feet firmly planted on the ground. You really get a feeling of smallness when you look at the magnitude of the task that has to be done. Sometimes it is frightening to realize that 120,000 people depend on you and your business. Whoever your board of directors are and whatever other safeguards you put into place, there comes a time when you have to make decisions that could eventually turn out to be fatal for the company. Nothing comes easily. If the choices are so terrifying, it is because you never have all the pertinent points of information in hand when you make a decision. The head of a business has to navigate in a fog of uncertainty. He is forced to take action in real-life circumstances, and that is precisely where the problem lies. Once again, at the root of every decision, there is the following question: Is it useful for the customer? Yes, because it is that which leads to the shareholders and customers being satisfied.

YVES MESSAROVITCH: Do you have a feeling that you still own your own name, when it falls like this into the public domain?

61

FRANÇOIS MICHELIN: My grandfather told me once that he was quite sorry that he had dubbed our tires "Michelin" tires. This aspect weighs heavily on a family. People never look at François. They look at Michelin. The only advantage that I see is that it gives a more human dimension to the product.

YVES MESSAROVITCH: When you give your products your own name, are you not also committing yourself to both your customers and your employees? In a way, you are giving them an additional guarantee. . . .

FRANÇOIS MICHELIN: Certainly. Having your name involved does, perhaps, add a dimension and even more than that, no doubt. It is an incentive for a person not to do too many stupid things!

IVAN LEVAÏ: It is interesting to see how widespread "signature" products are in the automotive world: Citroën, Peugeot, Renault, Ford. All these name brands are reminiscent of individuals and families.

FRANÇOIS MICHELIN: The automobile is a passion. No doubt, that is the reason for this!

As always, a person or a group of people constitutes the foundation of all progress. Most often these individuals and families have acted with a great deal of strength and courage in all sorts of circumstances.

IVAN LEVAÏ: Nowadays, businesses are no longer referred to by name but by abbreviations and initials. How do you explain the dropping of those names as a point of reference?

FRANÇOIS MICHELIN: At the beginning of the Industrial Age, bankers first put their trust in a man or a group of people. There was no such thing yet as public limited companies. At the beginning, the Peugeot family, for example, was a limited partnership, as we are.

YVES MESSAROVITCH: At the time, many businesses first started locally. Bankers and their families had long been rubbing shoulders with industrialists and their families. They had a well-known code of ethics, a common social and family environment, and a certain set of political convictions. Wasn't the consensus that existed at that time a factor contributing toward business stability?

FRANÇOIS MICHELIN: Certainly. Every venture has as its point of departure the desire that people have to build something together. That is how businesses start, on a local level, because certain individuals feel that, by joining together their efforts, they may be useful to society. In our present world, it is absolutely essential for us to rediscover not only the necessary legal structures but all the other means we need, as well, in order to preserve the factors that are vital for starting up a business and then promoting its growth. The form of corporate arrangement that Michelin enjoys, namely, a partnership limited by shares, is just such a means perhaps. Because of the statutory responsibility of the partners, you think twice before making any decision, while you try to discern whether such a decision carries any advantages in terms of the future.

IVAN LEVAÏ: Society as a whole has become impersonal in comparison to the one in which you grew up. The development of today's child takes place in an obscure system administered by faceless officials where "a nice piece of work" is no longer recognized and acknowledged as it once was. In spite of all this, have you tried to hand on the values that you hold dear to your children?

FRANÇOIS MICHELIN: My wife and I have tried to put our children in contact with matter, reality, and with nature, to allow them to experiment on their own. A father learns a lot more from his children than his children learn from him. Children ask marvelous questions. You think that you know, and then you realize that you cannot produce an explanation. Your mind has a constant tendency to operate in terms of a grand hierarchy, going from highest to lowest. This is a fundamental error. A little six-month-old child can teach you loads of things. Look at him in his stroller: There he is in his royal splendor, surveying the scene with wide-open eyes....

IVAN LEVAÏ: All the same, is there a guiding principle that the Michelins pass on to one another from father to son?

FRANÇOIS MICHELIN: Perhaps what we pass on is the perennial concern to be close to the facts. It is the sense of facts. Thus, we learn to love the product to the point where it becomes a thing that is pretty-near tyrannical. When you really love something, you sniff out anything that is not satisfactory, and it becomes unacceptable. Genetically, we are fiercely attached to the notion of service both to our country and to our customers, employees, and shareholders. Finally, I am not terribly enamored of the notion of the customer being the king. You cannot always discuss matters with a king. And you have to be able to discuss things, in order to reach an understanding. You cannot do anything with a customer who says, "Get lost!" So, you have to find a way for him to say "yes" to you. And this is only possible if what you are offering him corresponds to what he needs. A shoe salesman, even the most charming shoe salesman in the world, will never sell shoes that hurt your feet because the shoes are too narrow.

Another one of our passions is innovation. Technical innovation, of course, but there are other areas as well. The history of the business is a good illustration of this.

I might also add that, for generations, we have felt a deep respect for materials. Want an example? At the beginning of the century, people were doing research on a new electrical insulator that could be used instead of wood and ceramics. Wood soaked up water and caused short circuits. As for ceramics, they could not be worked properly. One of the company's engineers had the idea of producing ebonite with rubber and sulphur. This made for an outstanding rigid insulator that could be easily worked. It was an extraordinary discovery, but my grandfather decided not to develop the product. For him, it was absolutely inconceivable that one could harden the only elastic molecule on earth that occurs naturally. It was out of respect for the material that he made his decision. Shortly afterward, Bakelite appeared on the scene—an excellent insulator made with very inexpensive raw materials—formol and casein.

This attitude is of fundamental importance when you deal with people. The company must find the means to make it possible for each person's predominant trait to be brought out. It must also give each person the opportunity to become what he is. You cannot imagine the number of people who come to us as a chemical engineer or whatever, and who, after a few years, reorient themselves into an utterly different line of work because they discover, deep down in their guts, that they are also cut out for a lot of other things, over and above what they had originally thought. When you manage a company like ours, you have to be sufficiently flexible in your dealings with people in the organization so that each person, in his turn, can be "pneumatic," an "all-terrain tire," able to hug the road in any kind of weather.

IVAN LEVAÏ: Were the Michelin brothers, who founded the business, already committed to these values?

FRANÇOIS MICHELIN: As far as I know, yes, but the one who was most imbued with them was Edouard Michelin. "Your number-one task is to love the employees for whom you are responsible," he told his managers. To love people like this is, by no means, a kind of idiotic sentimentality. Quite simply, it means: Seeing people as they are.

IVAN LEVAÏ: No company director would venture to say this to one of his managers today.

FRANÇOIS MICHELIN: Do you think so? Mind you, when nowadays people use the term *human resources*, something happens to the concept of man.

IVAN LEVAÏ: Was your grandfather a Christian?

FRANÇOIS MICHELIN: Yes. Christianity explains why things are as they are. But is not any human being who stands in wonder before the beauty of a rose or a landscape a believer without knowing it? *"Beauty" is another name for God.* Many people do not want to follow their beliefs through to their logical conclusion, because of fear, perhaps, of the moral demands that might be made on them. These demands, I should mention in passing, concern the way that human beings coexist in harmony.

YVES MESSAROVITCH: Is that why there has always been an objective consensus among people, based on the hope that in the end things may turn out well?

FRANÇOIS MICHELIN: Yes. But that is not enough. Pascal said it quite well: "The man who commits suicide is looking for happiness." This shows to what depths of uncertainty and darkness the human conscience can sometimes plunge.

IVAN LEVAÏ: You are the product of an industrial dynasty that has attempted, throughout the process of your education, to pass on values to you. What age were you when you really accepted and acknowledged these values? When did you understand the nature of the company and its finality?

FRANÇOIS MICHELIN: At the outset, you know, my dream was not to run the company. I wanted to be a meteorologist! I do not know why, but clouds fascinate me. In my youth I embarked on studies for a diploma in meteorology at the Sorbonne.[1] I have quite vivid memories of my professor. He wanted us to share his passion for whirlwinds and other mysteries of the atmosphere. It was simply marvelous.

YVES MESSAROVITCH: Why study meteorology and not astrophysics?

FRANÇOIS MICHELIN: Once again, only because I find clouds fascinating.

IVAN LEVAÏ: It is such a chancy, uncertain thing to study.

FRANÇOIS MICHELIN: Precisely, that is what is so fascinating about it! Do you know that certain clouds are hollow on the inside, like certain cheeses? It is amazing. But let us get back to your question. You spoke about a dynasty. I do not care for the idea very much. It conjures up the notion of external pressure being brought to bear on the thinking of a young man or a young woman. This kind of pressure leads to no good. There is nothing more dreadful than someone who wants his son to follow in his footsteps at all costs. The child does not find himself being valued for what he is but, rather, in terms of an idea that is imposed on him from the outside. This is quite unhealthy.

IVAN LEVAÏ: Could you have done something else other than work at Michelin?

FRANÇOIS MICHELIN: Mr. Mignol, the inventor of the radial tire, once said to me: "If you do not like tires, get out of here!"

YVES MESSAROVITCH: Could a person really speak so directly like that to a member of the Michelin family?

FRANÇOIS MICHELIN: Yes. It is one of the characteristic features of the company. The best ideas do not necessarily come from the boss. The best idea is the one that best satisfies the customer. This attitude is genetically ingrained in our company.

YVES MESSAROVITCH: So you were captivated by tires?

66 *Chapter Five*

FRANÇOIS MICHELIN: What a fascinating object! The car is a marvelous symbol that epitomizes the whole history of humanity all on its own: the marathon, Roman roads, the horse.

IVAN LEVAÏ: How old were you when you were taken by this passion?

FRANÇOIS MICHELIN: I do not know. It is as if you were asking me how old I was when I felt like breathing. When you ask a centipede how he manages to walk, do you know what happens? He has a stroke.

YVES MESSAROVITCH: Have your children ever questioned their membership in the Michelin family? Have they disputed it at some point or other in their lives? Have they, for their part, tried to put distance between themselves and your work?

FRANÇOIS MICHELIN: At times, they found my work annoying because it was taking me away a bit too much.

IVAN LEVAÏ: Do they want to follow in your footsteps one day?

FRANÇOIS MICHELIN: Yes. When you are young and you hear people talking about a fascinating job all the time, you develop an interest in it. They grew up in Clermont, and they recognize the importance of the company. They have also seen people on strike marching past our house. This has certainly left its mark on them.

IVAN LEVAÏ: Did the context of class struggle, which was prominent at the time you were a child, leave its mark on you?

FRANÇOIS MICHELIN: I remember a day in the year 1936 when, while I was with my grandfather in his office on Cours Sablon, a long line of people on strike passed beneath our windows.[2] When I heard some noise, I went to the window and lifted up the curtain, which prompted shouting. My grandfather said to me: "People will tell you that these people are nasty, but that is not true." I realized that my grandfather was speaking the truth, which leads me to say that the notion of class struggle stems from an intellectual laziness in which people want to avoid asking themselves real questions.

Since that time, I have been haunted by this phrase of his: "If you regard a Communist as a class enemy, you are making a mistake. If you see him as a man who simply has a way of thinking that is different from yours, that is a totally different matter." Each time I meet someone, I ask myself: *What diamond is hidden in this person?* All these jewels that surround us make an incredible crown, when we have learned how to open our eyes and see them.

IVAN LEVAÏ: Do you think in the same way when you cross paths with Mrs. Martine Aubry, our current minister of employment and solidarity?

FRANÇOIS MICHELIN: Of course. My personal experience has shown me that it is difficult for people to accept this notion of the diamond in terms of their own lives. If you look closely at this hidden jewel, it reveals many things to you, both good and bad. Similarly, the attitude of the people around you tells you an enormous number of things.

YVES MESSAROVITCH: In your opinion, why do certain people look at their "jewel" but do not have enough confidence in it, preferring to bow to a preestablished system?

FRANÇOIS MICHELIN: They do not follow the implications of their reasoning right to its logical end. They fail to draw the right conclusions about it. If the three of us find it possible to have a conversation together, it is because each of us looks on the other person as being unique, a self-given entity, not reducible to any other. It is only under this kind of conditions that you can build something.

IVAN LEVAÏ: But let us get back down to earth here. Michelin has, with the utmost secrecy, developed a new machine that bears the mysterious name of "C3M." According to the information that one hears here and there, this great invention allows a considerable increase in productivity. Are you not building a dangerous world where the technology of production is going to get the upper hand over man in a lasting, permanent way?

FRANÇOIS MICHELIN: To launch an average factory costs a billion francs and takes four years. With C3M you put the machine in place, and three days later, it is producing tires! It is a fantastic invention, which will be able to be used in any so-called developing country, allowing those who use it to pass directly into the twenty-first century.

YVES MESSAROVITCH: But it will only use a highly skilled workforce.

FRANÇOIS MICHELIN: People have the wrong idea whenever they talk about skilled labor. You know, people have a phenomenal capacity to move forward and make progress.

YVES MESSAROVITCH: As regards technological innovation, Michelin has always been at the forefront: the radial tire, the secret new C3M process, the green tire, the PAX System,[3] the marvelous sensors that transmit tire pressure readings right to the dashboard. . . . Who is behind all these inventions? Is it the fruit of the work of licensed engineers charged with the job of "making discoveries," or, on the contrary, do you encourage spontaneous innovation?

FRANÇOIS MICHELIN: It seems to me that innovation is always spontaneous if the human environment is favorable. Good ideas can be conceived anywhere: in the workshop, in the office, with customers, et cetera. It is up to those in charge of research departments to surround themselves with engineers who have the humility to implement ideas that are not necessarily theirs. As for the boss, sometimes he has to go against the reservations that some of the people in his work-force might have. When we were ready to launch the green tire, some of the people in the company were opposed to it. They argued that the machinery would have to be changed and that it was going to cost a lot. But, along with Mr. Zingraff,[4] we held firm, for the facts of the matter showed that this was an excellent product and that, among its other advantages, it consumed less energy. To move a one-ton car forward, you need twelve kilos of force/cm^2 with a regular tire, but only eight kilos with a green tire. It is an ecological tire!

IVAN LEVAÏ: Nevertheless, by developing your revolutionary C3M machine, you are well-aware that you are helping to give birth to a world in which, twenty years hence, there will not be any work. . . .

FRANÇOIS MICHELIN: What is work, Mr. Levaï?

IVAN LEVAÏ: It is that human activity, be it intellectual or manual, that allows something to be done; it allows a person's talents to bear fruit.

FRANÇOIS MICHELIN: That is why, when you are on vacation, there is nothing to keep you from working. At the same time, as some occupations die off, others are emerging. Why do you suppose that development and progress should have an end term placed on them? In the nineteenth century, who would have thought that a day would come when the service economy and research sector would create more employment than industry does?

We should make note of something here: Does not the tediousness of work also stem from the fact that our pride is forced to submit not only to the reality of inanimate materials but, above all, to the reality that is inherent to man? Is not the sweat of our brow often a by-product of our battered pride?

Notes and Explanations

1. Sorbonne: Paris university created in 1257; famous for its literature, philosophy, languages, and theology curriculum.
2. Cours Sablon: One of the large avenues in Clermont-Ferrand, where Edouard Michelin used to live.
3. PAX System: One of the latest inventions of the Michelin group, which proposes a system that allows one to drive safely with a flat tire and, thus, to suppress the spare wheel.
4. René Zingraff (1937–): One of the three managing partners of the Michelin group. He assumed the position in 1986.

6

And Why Not?

IVAN LEVAÏ: How do you manage to reconcile your Christian humanism with capitalism?

FRANÇOIS MICHELIN: The word *capitalism* was born in Marx's mind. He could only see the relationship between capital and labor as a form of fight to the death, which he dubbed "the class struggle." With his Hegelian verbosity, he thus justified hatred as the mainspring of history; but capital is for business what the hull of his ship is for the sailor.[1] The essential role of the capitalist consists of constantly seeing to it that the hull of the ship allows business to sail as far as possible without ever taking on water. Why should there be a fight to the death between capital and labor? The two of them are as inseparable as the hand and the brain. The dialecticians are a pain, always being on the lookout for division everywhere. Consider a rabbit: It has paws, a head, a tail, and it is alive. If, on the one hand, you analyze the paws and then go on from there to analyze the head, that is the end of the rabbit! Descartes is in total error when he applies his dualism to human life! Too much analysis kills life.

As for Marx, it has been proven that he was incapable of understanding the essential role of capital. It is a fundamental failing of dialectical materialism to be always mistaking consequences for causes. Marxism is utterly deluded about objectives. If Karl Marx had lived with ship captains, he would not have invented the word *capitalism* but, rather, *hullism*. . . . He had absolutely no understanding of the role that shareholders play.

Nevertheless, there is something else behind the word *capitalism*. We have already spoken about it. You have men and women, and they have their own responsibilities and autonomy, which need to be defended constantly against the invasion of the State and society. When certain financial aspects of capitalism are criticized, what is being attacked, in fact, are the means necessary for the freedom of persons. Once again, the fundamental question is whether man is a subject or an object, whether society is for man or man for society, and whether we should opt for liberal capitalism or collectivism.

IVAN LEVAÏ: When you are a Christian employer, what should your basic outlook on globalization be?

FRANÇOIS MICHELIN: According to you, what does being Christian mean?

IVAN LEVAÏ: Someone who considers himself to have a responsibility toward humanity.

FRANÇOIS MICHELIN: And what about yourself? Do you not share this feeling?
On a deeper level, the Christian way of thinking, when it is analyzed dispassionately, is the only one that gives every man and every woman answers to their most profound questions and does so in a spirit of tremendous respect for their freedom.

IVAN LEVAÏ: But you are not an employer like any other. You have ethics and morality.

FRANÇOIS MICHELIN: You know, every person walks his own path and has his own set of experiences. The system of ethics—to respond somewhat more fully to an earlier question—that my Christian faith gives me is formidable, since it is constantly showing me the gap that exists between what I am doing and what I *should* be doing. But at the same time, it gives me the strength to carry on.

IVAN LEVAÏ: But are you not boxing yourself in, because you intend to respect the rules of fair play and loyalty that others, inevitably, do not care to impose on themselves?

FRANÇOIS MICHELIN: *Sooner or later, a person pays the consequences for what he has said or done.* Christian or not, if you accept this reality, you act with a clear conscience. Christian faith adds something to the equation, as it explains why the world is ordered as it is. It shows the basic attitude that we should have, in order to grow and to help others to grow. Perhaps a Christian has a more detailed vision of things, because it is more natural for him to go to the very foundations of man. In my opinion, this is what makes the difference on the human level.

IVAN LEVAÏ: Is not Christianity a moral system that invites us to make a better apportionment of the fruits and profits of business? Consider Jesus' parable at the Sea of Galilee—the sharing of the bread and the fish.

FRANÇOIS MICHELIN: Most certainly.

I should point out to you that the sharing of the bread and the fish is not a parable but a historical action. Before it was shared, the bread had to be multiplied. Isn't this precisely where the skill of the industrialist lies?

Christianity has put man back at the very heart of the world. Respect for the other person is part of the Christian way of thinking—but how weak we feel, faced with this objective!

YVES MESSAROVITCH: Certain Christian employers have left a distinctive stamp on the inner workings of their business and have tried to express their convictions in the way that they have organized human relationships. Isn't the growth of global competition going to force these businesses to become common, everyday companies?

FRANÇOIS MICHELIN: In itself, globalization constitutes a formidable measuring tool. If, in the last fifteen years, we have had to part with many people in the group, it is not because of globalization but because of obstacles that have been put in the way of progressive adaptation. It is also one of the consequences of the unrealistic growth that occurred in the boom period following World War II. As a whole, our personnel understood the reasons for our reductions in overall staff. One day, when I was discussing things with our employees in a workshop, a union representative from the CGT said to me: "Mr. François, we are well-aware that, if you let people go, it is because you really do not have any other choice."[2] He was right. Over and above offering early retirement programs, we have made substantial efforts, with success, to help a great number of people find new jobs.

IVAN LEVAÏ: Whether they are Christians or not, many employers share the same values. That is all well and good, but globalization gives consumers access to products made on the other side of the world by people who do not necessarily respect the same set of ethics and whose social systems can be very different. How do you know, in this great, open, global marketplace, whether you are buying products made by underpaid workers who do not even operate within a rudimentary, supportive social framework?

FRANÇOIS MICHELIN: "Underpaid"—relative to whom and what? A country's economy is a seamless whole. It is dangerous to pick out one element of it and compare it to an external situation. The question of globalization lies within these parameters. That being said, people are far from being perfect. Every person is responsible for the way he buys and consumes.

YVES MESSAROVITCH: All the same, there is an information problem.

FRANÇOIS MICHELIN: Either you are passive and you do not ask yourself any questions, or else you demonstrate your dignity and you ask yourself questions. There is nothing more formative than a free act of buying.

IVAN LEVAÏ: Because of mergers and concentrations of power, dominant groups can be seen to be emerging, and they exercise a form of dictatorship over the market. When the fox has eaten all the chickens and he rules the roost, what happens then? Are each of the actors in a capitalist society (shareholder, customer, worker) still sure that they will reap the just rewards for their efforts?

FRANÇOIS MICHELIN: This is where the State must intervene. It is up to the State to guarantee a healthy currency and to make sure that dominant positions are not used improperly. Just as you need a highway code, you need strict, simple rules guaranteeing that no business (or group of businesses) can ever lay down the law to the market. Capitalism can only function if every customer is in a position to make a free and responsible choice. By not respecting this freedom, people are eventually weakened and undermined.

YVES MESSAROVITCH: Even so, you can be dominant without exercising a monopoly.

FRANÇOIS MICHELIN: Exactly. We have to take the initiative in imposing limits on ourselves, even though our pride may point us in an opposite direction. The word *dominant* comes from the Latin *dominus*, which means "the man of the house." Have you ever seen "the man of the house" take the tiles off his roof in order to get running water in his bathroom! Anyone who cares about his house strives for harmonious additions and renovations. If you do not take the truth of the market into account, you are making a mistake.

IVAN LEVAÏ: In your view, the State should make sure that certain laws are respected, but more and more we are seeing the growth of a form of capitalism that knows no borders and shows utter disdain for the laws and injunctions issued by countries.

FRANÇOIS MICHELIN: This international openness is by definition a necessary thing. Let us not forget that we have to go abroad to buy raw materials that cannot be found on our own soil, beginning with oil. The French economy has to be global or it will no longer exist! Nor is it possible any longer for us to keep away from the scientific research that is taking place in the world. The globalization of technical discovery and thought is a given that we have to accept in order to move forward and make progress.

YVES MESSAROVITCH: But what if you are compelled to do things a certain way to gain a foothold in a geographical area? If your competitors are doing these sorts of things, would you give up a market on account of moral reasons?

FRANÇOIS MICHELIN: Absolutely. There are limits that need to be respected. I believe that many "capitalists" are in agreement with me, but once again, let us stop rejecting globalization! I see it, rather, as a reason for hope that the French economy will evolve in the good sense of the term. Whom does globalization bother the most? The French State, which is going to have to admit—kicking and screaming—that it was mistaken to keep a system going that today is no longer viable. Our archaic systems of thought will not be a match much longer for the realities that are being brought home to us by the success of the Americans and the British. France is going to have to change. If not, she will die.

IVAN LEVAÏ: Much has been said about the success of a liberalized England, and now we discover that, in our day and age, five hundred thousand British children work in intolerable conditions. What should be done to combat this?

FRANÇOIS MICHELIN: If this is true, is it not the result of shortcomings on the part of the politicians? Is it not also fundamentally a problem of excessive costs? And what was happening twenty-five years ago? But, beyond that, let us also point out that capitalism is a reflection of man, and that is why it is a mixture of things that are both good and bad. As Churchill once said about democracy, "It is the worst form of government—except for all those other forms of government." Nevertheless, it is a system that works, because eventually it puts everyone face-to-face with his responsibilities. This is how humanity moves forward and makes progress.

YVES MESSAROVITCH: Nevertheless, there is a sort of hybrid position that has appeared between capitalism and Marxism, called "the mixed economy." Public opinion seems to love it, or French public opinion does, at any rate. This system maintains the illusion that public enterprise can do things as well as private enterprise without its disadvantages, such as layoffs, not to mention wage freezes. What link do you see between a mixed economy and Marxism?

FRANÇOIS MICHELIN: You cannot have two types of power base in a country, one of them responsible and the other irresponsible, especially if you ask one part of the population to pay for the irresponsibility of those who run the public-service sector. Once and for all, the State has to understand that it is not its job to manage the economy. The collusion that takes place between government and the public-service sector is much too dangerous.

IVAN LEVAÏ: At Michelin everything is concrete and down-to-earth. You manufacture a product that everybody knows and uses every day. You and your family are personally responsible for the future of your business because of its status as a limited partnership that involves your own property. Here you have developed a capitalism that is less offensive than the variety of capitalism that is a virtual monster, cloaked in anonymity, where you do not know who does what, who produces what.

FRANÇOIS MICHELIN: What you say needs to be qualified. You must never lose sight of the fact that money can only yield a profit when it is put at the service of mankind. Perhaps this is where Michelin's strength lies. How many times I have reiterated to our financiers that the figures are merely the fruits of the labor of men and women who have done their jobs all their lives, in order to work for themselves and for the success of the company. One day, to my great surprise, it was one of the workers who had the courage to tell them [the financiers] in the middle of a shareholders' meeting: "It is Mr. Michelin who is right, not you. Why can't you just let us work in peace?!"

IVAN LEVAÏ: Faced as you are with the problems that are undermining France and discouraging huge numbers of businessmen and workers, have you ever had the temptation to sell Michelin?

FRANÇOIS MICHELIN: No. My first reaction is to ask myself: *What can be done to get this country back on its feet again?* Besides, how do you expect me to walk away from the company and its people? When you are aware of all the humanity that sparkles in the eyes and faces of the men and women who work in the company, you do not ask yourself this kind of question.

YVES MESSAROVITCH: Do you think that, with time, progress has been made in changing the mind-set that people have? Are people doing more to adjust their thinking to the long-term rather than to the short-term?

FRANÇOIS MICHELIN: A great many of the company's employees know that the thirty-five-hour workweek law is based on ideas that are completely unrealistic. People do not have the courage to say that the more you work, the less unemployment you will have. If push comes to shove, people should be prepared to work a forty-one-hour workweek for thirty-nine hours of pay, in order to pull us out of this mess. Within two years the economy would pick up again, cost would be lowered, purchasing power would be increased, and workers would have to be hired, in order to meet the new production needs. These days, France is kept going only because the dollar is high, but nobody is to say that one of these days it may not fall to five francs to a dollar. If it drops while our costs rise, we will not be able to sell anything. Frankly, the imposed reduction of work time is an aberration and one more illustration of a vision that is too short-term and characterized by an ignorance of what work is.

One of the causes of the defeat of 1940 was the transition in 1936 from a forty-eight-hour workweek to one of forty hours. It became necessary to hire additional workers who could not be trained in time. This was evident in the armament sector where years are needed to train skilled personnel.

YVES MESSAROVITCH: The Germans also put people in their munitions plants who did not know what they were doing.

FRANÇOIS MICHELIN: Yes, but that was three or four years earlier. And they worked ten hours a day, six days a week. Besides, they had tutors who were responsible for passing on their know-how to the younger generation. The notion of apprenticeship has deep roots in Germany's industrial culture.

IVAN LEVAÏ: The production management systems that you are implementing at Michelin are good, no doubt, because they promote increased productivity, but the question is, Do they contribute to increased employment?

FRANÇOIS MICHELIN: Every process that contributes to a reduction in cost is beneficial. Many people would like to buy high-quality tires, but give up if they are too expensive. Every drop in prices contributes to a smoothly running economy. In France, people do not understand this yet. Why does the road tax on luxury cars remain exorbitant, even in the case of secondhand vehicles? Lots of people might toy with the idea of buying themselves a nice second- or thirdhand car for around twenty or thirty thousand francs, but they give up on the idea because of the additional expense arising from the road tax. What reason is there for their dreams and aspirations to be penalized other than a jealously hostile attitude that encourages the belief that the class struggle is actually still a going concern?

IVAN LEVAÏ: In your opinion, what is the urgency? Is it tax reform?

FRANÇOIS MICHELIN: We need to start by reducing the weight of government's hefty hand on the GDP. We are already at a figure between 50 and 60 percent in this respect and, in fact, these figures are increasing rather than decreasing. Is it a solution to hire more government employees for purely political reasons and give them a higher rate of pay? At the same time, they have announced to productive workers in the private sector that in order to "amortize" the consequences of giving thirty-nine hours of pay for a thirty-five-hour workweek, they will need to impose a three-year wage freeze! This is a serious inequality—and, also, a great way to slow down growth, since the salaries of government employees come from taxes.

You know, some government employees are not at ease with the situation. Remember the words of Proudhon: "Government employees, don't you ever forget that the money you live on is tax money!"[3]

After that, it will be possible to launch a reform of the tax structure, whose goal should be to facilitate growth. You know, many government employees think as I do and cannot understand the politicians.

IVAN LEVAÏ: The governments have come and gone, one after the other, and they all have the same obsession: namely, the reduction of unemployment. Sometimes you get the impression that all the recipes have been tried and that, at the same time, the range of possibilities gets narrower and narrower. They cannot play around with inflation or devaluation anymore. Yet, nobody has the courage to tackle an in-depth reform of our tax system. Is not the introduction of a shorter workweek the only solution that is somewhat innovative?

FRANÇOIS MICHELIN: Implementing a shorter workweek amounts to a unilateral imposition of increased business costs, which includes a raise in the hourly working wage. It is an absolute certainty that there will be more unemployed workers in France. Instead of saying to people: "Keep fighting the good fight. You will get out of this mess!" they are told: "You are going to die, but put your mind at ease—you will not even notice what is happening." Let us be realistic. We are headed right into great upheavals! And it will not be the fault of the down-to-earth, practical-minded employers.

YVES MESSAROVITCH: Are not the young people one of the potential vehicles for this revolution? France finds itself at a dramatic crossroads. One out of every four young people who are looking for a job cannot find one.

FRANÇOIS MICHELIN: I see two reasons for this. The first stems from a distorted sense of discernment on the part of qualified young people with degrees who have been told that they cannot do any other job except what they have been trained to do. And they have been told that it is better to be a government employee than to produce, because producing in the private sector is "shameful." There is a second reason: their total ignorance of the way that business works.

Our personnel department implemented a program called "Springboard for Youth," in which 190 sponsors, active or retired members of the company, drawn from different disciplines, explain their work to young people and tell them what life in industry is all about. In a year, this experiment made it possible for more than three hundred young people to find work. At the plant in Vannes,[4] we duplicated the same experiment with people who did not have work and were in dreadful psychological shape. Today, thanks to the dedication of their sponsors and the work they themselves have done, they have been transformed. To the great joy of their sponsors, they have rediscovered their dignity.

These are the types of initiatives that carry the promise of success in resolving the problem of unemployed young people. In this way, they are given contact with reality.

As soon as things become official and thus loaded with rules and regulations, they are thought of as something that is owed, something that has to be, and this is how you start getting perverse side effects. If only they could take the shackles off and let us do what we have to do in a spirit of continuous adaptation! These programs that we have put in place for young people cost us fifty million francs a year. They demand time and generosity on the part of the people who work in the plant. The labor regulations we were faced with were absolutely paralyzing, but there was nothing that we could do about them; but, even in the government administration there are people with a heart, willing to make all this possible. This is a very hopeful sign for the future. We are walking hand in hand in the fight against unemployment.

IVAN LEVAÏ: In your eyes, is this sort of moral sponsorship of young people a solution for the future?

FRANÇOIS MICHELIN: If moral standards are the "operation manual" we use to direct us through life, yes.

IVAN LEVAÏ: I would rather put it in terms of passing on responsibilities. You have received a talent, you have made it bear fruit, and now you are giving a young person the means and resources to do the same.

FRANÇOIS MICHELIN: All of life's beauty can be fitted into this process. It lies at the heart of life in society. You are quite right.

IVAN LEVAÏ: Are you a pessimist or an optimist? Do you believe in progress? Is the situation better today than it was in your grandfather's time? And will it be better when your son assumes control of the company?

FRANÇOIS MICHELIN: Of course, I believe in progress. As for the situation today, it is difficult to make comparisons. The situations are not at all the same. When I arrived at the company, the radial tire technology was already in place. All I did was make use of it to allow Michelin to assume a relatively important place in the world. I found a team of outstanding men and women in place, and they taught me everything. The only thing that I really did was to give each one of them the means to release their personal energy. Believe me, though, this is a challenging but thrilling task—and it is the only way that I have been able to make decisions.

YVES MESSAROVITCH: This is what you call "being duty-bound to experiment."

FRANÇOIS MICHELIN: Have I been able to cope with things despite being saddled with the formidable weight of government regulations, not to mention all sorts of other constraints? Lost time is one of the reasons for this book, which is supposed to be a personal testimonial. When I was handed the responsibility for Michelin, an old hand, whom I have never forgotten, told me: "Be who you are, do not try to be your father or your grandfather. Be genuine, with all your strengths and weaknesses, but open your eyes, open them wide. Go into the workshops." Our so-called modern world is swarming with ideologists. It is going to be shattered by the impact of facts and reality. This will be a painful thing, but a source of progress.

YVES MESSAROVITCH: So you are more a pessimist then?

FRANÇOIS MICHELIN: If the pessimist is a person who says: "There is nothing we can do. We are going to crash into a brick wall," that is not me at all. If the optimist is a person who thinks that things will get straightened out on their own, I am not that, either. I think that you have to be a realist. You have to consider whether the lights that you are seeing are real lights and the shadows that you are seeing are real shadows. And you have to take action accordingly, basing yourself on a number of fundamental reflections on man's "necessary" freedom and the splendor of progress. Realism, I believe, is a characteristic trait of the industrialist who, of necessity, is an optimist, as he has to produce tangible results. At the heart of a life of action, reality rules.

And besides all this, there is something that I believe in that is, for me, a source of enthusiasm and confidence in the future: research. It digs into the whys and the wherefores of things and especially of people. It applies to every domain, including that of social relations. Research is an extraordinary training school for the human being and a powerful, unpredictable motor in the development of our modern societies. It is through research, as well, that you should teach people how to acquire a capacity for wonder.

IVAN LEVAÏ: My generation has lived through two incredible lies, Stalinism and Hitlerism. If, in the end, it was possible to overcome hardships like these, do you not think that our present-day difficulties can also be overcome one day? After all, they are just small problems when you consider the broad sweep of history.

FRANÇOIS MICHELIN: State planning is also a lie, a well-camouflaged one!

Yes, of course, these problems can be overcome. I know, through experience, that man has exceptional resources that come forth whenever difficulties arise. I have great confidence in human beings, a confidence that is based on real-life experience. All that man asks for is to be allowed to surpass himself and become what he is, as soon as you give him the means to do so and you acknowledge all the glorious splendor of his humanity. Any man that you can look at straight in the face, regarding him as a unique individual who is free and responsible, blazes forth like a light as dazzling as any sun. When I think of everything that could be accomplished if one could release all the energy found in human beings!

IVAN LEVAÏ: Would Michelin be Michelin if its boss did not believe in God?

FRANÇOIS MICHELIN: The world is made up of mysteries that nobody can regard with indifference. Why do people have a human, emotional dimension of such great beauty? Why is technological progress limitless? Why is the world brimming over with vast streams of intelligence, as Einstein said? Did man create himself on his own? Is mind the product of matter or, on the contrary, can matter be perceived and comprehended by mind? If you agree to ask yourself these questions, you should follow the thread of their implications right to the end and read the Bible: the Gospels, the psalms, the proverbs, the texts of the Church. You will discover an answer that goes beyond the human intellect, but it is an answer that is meant to be savored, an answer that shines in the night like the North Star. God is unexplainable. He is said to be boundless, which simply means that he cannot be understood by our human mind. The greatest act that the intellect can engage in is to acknowledge its limits and to accept the mystery of things.

YVES MESSAROVITCH: At the same time, there is a vast coherence in infinity that remains unexplainable.

FRANÇOIS MICHELIN: God tells us that: "Without Me you can do nothing good and worthwhile, because I am the way, the truth, and the life." God is a mystery, but very much alive, deep inside each one of us, and he is calling us. He acts out of a tremendous respect for our freedom. We cannot cure ourselves any more than a doctor can operate on himself for appendicitis! The mystery of every human being, the mystery of God—the two of them call out to one another, you know. Nobody will ever succeed in putting people into an equation.

IVAN LEVAÏ: Has your faith, which is so sincere, changed the way life is lived in the company?

FRANÇOIS MICHELIN: God only knows, not I! But the criterion of whether life has been changed for the better in the company is the level of satisfaction achieved by those who constitute it, namely, the employees, the shareholders, and the customers.

And what progress still needs to be made!

With Joan of Arc I would say: "If I have faith, may God keep it and preserve it. If I do not have it, may God grant it to me."[5] But what is faith? A philosopher has said: "When you are in the presence of a friend, you are in the presence of a mystery, but you know through experience that this friend provides you with something. You believe in your friend, you have faith in your friend." Note that the object of faith is your friend and that faith is an act that binds you to your friend in a mysterious way.

IVAN LEVAÏ: Has your faith led you to surround yourself with people who share the same convictions as you do?

FRANÇOIS MICHELIN: If you are talking about religious convictions, I would say, no. What the plant needs and looks for in people is the soundness of their reasoning, their sense of reality, and their concern for others. Among people who call themselves "Christians," there are some who do not reason soundly, drawing on ready-made ideas and preconceptions, while others reason soundly and are sensitive to what is concrete and down-to-earth. It is the same with those who do not broadcast their convictions one way or another. *Christianity is a life, not an ideology.*

IVAN LEVAÏ: If you were to die tomorrow, would you feel that you had accomplished your task on earth?

FRANÇOIS MICHELIN: Who can claim to have accomplished his task? A person never stops being enriched by his association with others and, although he does not know it, he enriches them in return. Anyone who dies in full consciousness cannot but have the feeling that he has all kinds of things left to do yet. As you age, you begin to notice with some degree of calmness and equanimity that you have not been of much use.

YVES MESSAROVITCH: What message would you like to pass on to your son?

FRANÇOIS MICHELIN: "Truth is greater than you are," my grandfather once said to me. And he added: "The truth is hidden among the facts, just like precious metal in a load of ore." In essence, truth resides in a right relationship to reality. *The task of acting on the truth is never finished.*

In addition to this, I would also say, "Be loving." To love someone is to accept that person as he or she is, it is to go in search of the plain, unvarnished truth about that person and to acknowledge this truth, whatever it may be, even if it is unexplainable. Time and time again people have said to me: "You cannot make me believe that!" And my answer to them is: "It is not my job to make you believe it, but it is my job to tell it to you." What it amounts to is, simply, a respect for the freedom of the person. It is a respect for the mystery of the person.

Furthermore, nobody knows what his children's mission in life will be.

IVAN LEVAÏ: You demonstrate a humility that stands in great contrast to the arrogance of many politicians.

FRANÇOIS MICHELIN: Are they really arrogant? It is my opinion, rather, that we have not been able to convey to them our practical experience of life. Let me reiterate: Have we been able to make them understand that the customer is not a taxpayer, that the customer is the reason for the existence of the business? There is nobody more humble than a peasant or, more generally speaking, those who are in contact with the real and the concrete. In the company, people on the shop floor do an outstanding, indeed, extraordinary, job every day. And yet, what fantastic humility they have in their eyes! It is wrong to put down manual labor, especially as it demands such careful attention to detail, such dogged tenacity. An engineer once said to me: "During my studies I was not taught that workers could be intelligent, too." It is crazy—the number of foolish ideas that are planted in the minds of our young graduates and left to fester there! That engineer was looking at the job, not the man.

This brings to mind a personal experience. When I was a young shop manager, it was suggested that I accept a man from another workshop who was, himself, also young. He had a bad reputation both with regard to his behavior and to his work. Of course, I spoke about him to Mr. Marchand, who was teaching me

And Why Not?   81

my job at the time: "Should this man be in such a critically important work-shop?" This is how he answered me: "Mr. François, you do not know this man, and remember that a man's reputation is not necessarily a fact. Forget everything that has been said about him." So I took him on and explained to him that there were three basic points that had to be heeded in the workshop: no accidents on the job; an attitude of faithful respect for our methods of operation, which is to say, a concern for quality; and finally, production. I added: "If you see that there are improvements to be made, by all means tell us." Three months later, he had one of the most sensitive jobs in the shop, and I never had the slightest problem with him. What a lesson!

YVES MESSAROVITCH: Since the Grenelle Accords in 1968 you have cho-sen to disappear from the scene and to give interviews only on rare occasions. Why haven't you wanted to do more to pass on these ideas that are so close to your heart?

FRANÇOIS MICHELIN: It is the fault of the journalists who have said to me: "The less you speak out, the more you will be heard." What is a person to do in that case? No, in the final analysis, a person needs time to reflect and mature. Perhaps I was mistaken. But would people have listened? When people are swamped with ready-made ideas, they are not too disposed to listen to practical ideas. You have to be hungry to eat. I am barely beginning to discover what we were made for and what I was made for. I am fascinated by the company, that is obvious. I love tires and cars, but that is not enough. What counts more than any-thing else is helping people to become what they are.

How difficult this is, though! Pascal says quite rightly: "How does it happen that lame people do not irritate us, while a lame mind does? It is because lame people are prepared to admit that we are walking straight, but a lame mind claims that we are the ones who are lame. Otherwise we would have pity on the person with the lame mind rather than being angry with him." I find this a haunting thought, whether I apply it to myself or to others.

Once, on a plane, I met a young manager who had just been hired by Michelin. I asked him why he had chosen to come to work for the company.

His answer to me was: "In the advertisement, it said that success on this job demanded good human qualities. That is what caught my eye."

I added: "The company is waiting for you to become what you are by culti-vating your qualities."

Notes and Explanations

1. Georg Hegel (1770–1831): German philosopher.
2. CGT: Confédération Générale du Travail, hard-core Marxist-Leninist, French trade union.

3. Pierre Joseph Proudhon (1809–1865): French anarchist who created the first mutuals.
4. Vannes: Small French town in the west of France where Michelin has a plant.
5. Saint Joan of Arc (1412–1431): Was divinely inspired to deliver France from the English invaders. She was condemned for sorcery and burned at the stake in English-controlled territory in Rouen. Patron saint of France.

POSTSCRIPT

The Five-Step Method

It is impossible, of course, to imagine being able to achieve a conclusive ending to a dialogue about people in society. The aspect of mystery that resides in every person *is* so great—but it is possible to set down areas of fundamental agreement that allow some imposition of structure on this symphony of ideas.

What follows is an internal memorandum written by Edouard Michelin in 1912 and known in the company as "The Five-Step Method." It rounds off, in a unique way, what we have spoken about.

Memorandum from Edouard Michelin
Regarding "The Five-Step Method"

A majority of the difficulties that arise in the company between men and between departments—not to mention a majority of the mistakes that are made—stem from the following causes, which the "five-step method" makes it possible to avoid almost every time:

(a) *When a question has not been formulated with sufficient clarity.* It is extremely rare for a question to be formulated properly right at the outset. You have to make clear where you are starting from. It can be said that a question that is properly formulated is a question that is halfway to being resolved.

(b) *When your investigation has not been thorough.* That is to say, when your reasoning has been done on the basis of incomplete facts. An investigation and analysis of the facts are of prime importance. Carnegie says that every time that he has lost money, it is because his investigation had been incomplete. If you look at the cathedral from rue des Gras, you see two spires on it.[1] When you are inside, you cannot see them anymore, but you see the nave instead. When you see a squad of soldiers coming out of a small street, you do not know if there is a regiment or a brigade following on its heels. So, do not initiate your reasoning process by taking the fact that you have only seen the squad as the basis of your reasoning.

(c) *When you have not considered all the possible solutions.* In fact, it is often the solution rejected out-of-hand that would have worked.

(d) *When you have adopted a solution without looking at all its disadvantages and dangers or its repercussions on other departments.* Therefore, what needs to be adopted is the system that I have used for a long time, which I call "the system based on the table of advantages and disadvantages" (see below).

(e) *When you have not considered the financial consequences.* It is our goal to produce the best tires at the best possible price.

The Method Based on the Table of Advantages Versus Disadvantages

Take a piece of paper and divide it into two columns. To the left, write down a complete, numbered list of advantages. To the right, write down a complete, numbered list of all the disadvantages. Make sure that you keep it all on one sheet. Once the list is made, you indicate with checkmarks the numbered points that you find the most worthwhile, and you lightly cross out the points of argu-

Advantages	Disadvantages
1. It requires questions to be formulated clearly and in a complete way.	1. It takes time (but this is not wasted time).
2. It requires a good inspection of every aspect of the question.	2. It is boring.
3. It requires a consideration of all the possible solutions.	
4. It allows one to foresee the dangers and thus to take precautions in advance against them.	
5. It leads to a search for the most economical solution, which is also generally the simplest and the fastest.	

ment that have been judged, upon closer examination, to be insignificant, making sure to keep them legible. This is an excellent tool that can help people get used to judge what constitutes a serious point of argument; that is to say, a point that needs to have a bearing on any decision that is made.

Conclusion: The Five-Step Method Is to Be Adopted

I ask you to apply this method. If the boss, for example, does not use it, make sure that you point out to him that he is not using a good and useful method. The Five-Step Method should be the benchmark for every action that takes place within the company.

FRANÇOIS MICHELIN: This note, a decision from the boss, in which he, no less than his workers, obliges himself to live by its dictates, is a perfect illustration of the process on which basis Michelin has sought to build its fortunes. I know of no area of life in which it cannot be applied. Its essential virtue is that it allows each person to express himself and so, to derive benefit from all the other minds that are tackling a problem. How else can a society that is truly free and responsible be constructed? This is closely akin to the major problem that arises, I believe, from that dilemma that we all have in common, which has always fascinated me: namely, the choice between subject and object, between person and individual. Though demanding, it is also a marvelous source of potential progress.

Note and Explanation

1. Rue des Gras: One of the small streets close to the Michelin plant in Clermont-Ferrand.

INDEX

87

ABOUT THE AUTHORS

FRANÇOIS MICHELIN began working at his family's firm in Clermont-Ferrand in 1951. He served there in various capacities before assuming in 1955 the responsibility of managing partner, from which he retired in 2002. His achievements include promoting the development of the radial tire, which revolutionized the tire industry and established Compagnie Générale des Etablissements Michelin (CGEM) as a global company and the world's largest tire manufacturer.

IVAN LEVAÏ and YVES MESSAROVITCH have spent many years working as journalists in France. Ivan Levaï is editorial director of *La Tribune*, and Yves Messarovitch writes in the business pages of *Le Figaro*.